The Price
of Admission

THOMAS J. KANE

The Price of Admission

Rethinking How Americans Pay for College

Brookings Institution Press / *Washington, D.C.*

Russell Sage Foundation / *New York, N.Y.*

The Price of Admission: Rethinking How Americans Pay for College
may be ordered from:

Brookings Institution Press
1775 Massachusetts Avenue, N.W.
Washington, D.C. 20036
Tel: 1-800/275-1447 or 202/797-6258
Fax: 202/797-6004
www.brookings.edu

Library of Congress Cataloging-in-Publication data

Kane, Thomas J.
The price of admission : rethinking how Americans pay for college /
Thomas J. Kane.
   p.   cm.
   ISBN 0-8157-5014-5 (cloth : alk. paper)
   ISBN 0-8157-5013-7 (pbk. : alk. paper)
   1. College costs—United States. 2. Student aid—United States.
3. Government aid to education—United States. 4. Parents—United
States. 5. Finance, Personal. I. Title.
   LB2342 .K35 1999   99-6357
   378.3'0973—dc2   CIP

9 8 7 6 5 4 3 2 1

The paper used in this publication meets the minimum requirements of the
American National Standard for Information Sciences—Permanence of
Paper for Printed Library Materials, ANSI Z39.48-1984.

Typeset in Palatino

Composition by R. Lynn Rivenbark
Macon, Georgia

Printed by R. R. Donnelley and Sons
Harrisonburg, Virginia

Acknowledgements

The seed for this book was planted ten years ago, as I was working on a dissertation on unemployment insurance receipt. One of my advisers, David Wise, suggested that the university's president, Derek Bok, needed a graduate student to study trends in college enrollment. For good or ill, I never turned back. Thanks to David for his generous stewardship and to Derek for asking the hard questions that have kept me busy all these years.

I also want to thank David Ellwood, my adviser, friend, and colleague of longest standing, whose counsel I have repeatedly sought over the past decade and a half. I recall as a first-year graduate student telling David that I would rather have an impact on how people thought about a public policy question than spend my career hammering at narrow empirical questions. I thank him for not having me expelled on the spot for drawing a distinction between the two.

At least once a year, I could count on receiving a phone call from Charles Clotfelter of the National Bureau of Economic Research's program on the economics of higher education, asking me if I had a paper to present. Many of the questions posed in this book grew out of papers originally presented at those conferences. Derek Bok got me started in this field, but if Charlie had not called so often, I might have drifted away from research on higher education and never written this book (although I might have finished that long-neglected dissertation on unemployment insurance).

Everywhere that I have worked—the Kennedy School, the Brookings Institution, and the President's Council of Economic Advisers—I have been blessed with brilliant friends to turn to when I am short on ideas or inspiration. For countless suggestions provided in the hallway or over a cup of tea, I must thank Douglas Staiger, William Dickens, Anne

Piehl, Dietmar Harhoff, and Jeff Liebman. Each listened to a series of undeveloped ideas and always helped improve them. A more complete list of the long-suffering contributors of suggestions for this book would include Larry Katz and Richard Murnane at Harvard; Cecilia Rouse at Princeton, Sarah Turner and Dave Breneman at the University of Virginia; Don Stewart of the College Board; Michael Ash, Peter Orszag and Louise Sheiner from the President's Council of Economic Advisers; and Henry Aaron, Barry Bosworth, Gary Burtless, Bill Gale, Helen Ladd, Charles Schultze, Robert Reischauer, and Lois Rice at Brookings. Thanks, as well, to Sandy Jencks for a series of particularly enlightening conversations over Indian food. Now that the book is done, maybe we should pick a new restaurant.

In addition to the insights of anonymous referees, the book has been much improved by the careful comments of Dan Madzelan, Michael McPherson, Morton Schapiro, Robert Shireman, Sarah Turner, Susan Dynarski, Sandra Baum, and William Bowen. I am deeply indebted to their willingness to help, often with little notice and even less compensation.

Dan Madzelan and Dave Bergeron of the Department of Education, and Jennifer Kron and Aromie Noe of the Office of Management and Budget patiently answered my countless questions about financial aid program rules (and graciously hid any embarrassment at my ignorance). Three research assistants—Lauren Brown, Rachel Deyette and Tony Shen—were wonderfully helpful and thankfully patient with me at various stages of the project. My assistant, Jean Reed, already knows that I could not function without her.

At the Brookings Institution, Jim Schneider, Jill Bernstein, and Tanjam Jacobson provided much-needed editorial assistance. Jennifer Eichberger scoured the text for factual errors and patiently reconciled the most obvious mistakes. Bob Elwood indexed the pages, and Vicki Chamlee proofread them.

I began work on this project while a visiting fellow in the Brown Center for Education Policy at the Brookings Institution. The Russell Sage Foundation generously supported the project. I thank Henry Aaron and Robert Litan at Brookings and Eric Wanner at Russell Sage for their patience. I also thank Fred Schauer and Julie Wilson at the Kennedy School of Government and William Bowen and Harriet Zuckerman at the Mellon Foundation for affording me the time to finish the project over the past year.

Like ice skating, writing a book requires a sense of momentum and the ability to persevere over occasional patches of thin ice. Unfortunately, by temperament, I am more comfortable plodding than skating. I would not have finished without the patient support of my wife and friend, Karen Grace Gray, who consistently suggested that I let go of the handrail and try again (for good reason, Grace is her middle name). I dedicate this book to my wise and generous parents, Richard and Mary Kane.

Contents

1

Introduction

During the past fifteen years the labor market has distributed ever larger rewards to workers who have college educations. In 1980 the average 25- to 34-year-old male college graduate earned 19 percent more than a male high school graduate of the same age. By 1995 the difference had widened to 52 percent. And the difference has not been restricted to those who complete a bachelor's degree. The earnings premium for people with some college compared with those holding only a high school degree has increased from 4 percent to 11 percent.[1]

Not coincidentally, as the rewards for educational attainment have grown, calls to reform the education system have become louder. Reformers have lobbied for improving the quality of elementary and secondary education through school choice, national achievement standards, greater accountability from individual schools, and a long list of other ideas.

Many of these proposals, particularly those that improve accountability and allow more school-level decisionmaking, may well have merit. But ever since the publication of *Equality of Educational Opportunity* in 1966 (commonly known as the Coleman Report), researchers and policymakers have argued about whether incremental increases in school spending and other school reform efforts have yielded improvements in student performance.[2] Indeed, many of those efforts have not been effective.

1. National Center for Education Statistics (1997a, p. 120).
2. Coleman and others (1966). For an insightful summary of the issues in that debate, see Burtless (1996).

1

The reader will be reassured to know that I do not plan to enter the fray over elementary and secondary school reform. Rather, my purpose is to explore a different focus for investing in education: targeting existing subsidies for higher education more effectively to allow young people to continue their training after high school. Relative to the arduous process of reforming elementary and secondary schools, reforming the way Americans pay for college may offer even better opportunities for swifter gains in labor market preparedness.

Education's Response to the Labor Market

It did not take long for many American parents and families to respond to the changing labor market conditions. Soon after the wage premiums for the college educated began to increase in the late 1970s, a flurry of reports such as *A Nation at Risk* sounded the alarm over declining test scores.[3] Since then, many states and local school districts have launched ambitious reform projects. A decade of these efforts has yielded progress.

— High school students are spending more time on homework. The proportion of 13-year-olds reporting that they had no homework or that they had not done their homework declined from 38 percent in 1979 to 27 percent in 1996.[4]

— The proportion of eleventh and twelfth grade students taking advanced placement courses grew by 175 percent between 1984 and 1995.[5]

— The average public high school graduate completed 53 percent more courses in algebra or higher mathematics, 40 percent more in science, and 8 percent more in English in 1994 than in 1982.[6]

— Between 1980 and 1993 the proportion of students in grades ten through twelve who remained in school grew for whites, blacks, and Hispanics.[7] The decline in dropout rates was particularly large for African Americans.

---

3. National Commission on Excellence in Education (1983).
4. The estimate for 1979 is drawn from Mullis and Jenkins (1990, table 3.4); the later figure is drawn from National Center for Education Statistics (1997b, table 109).
5. National Center for Education Statistics (1997a, p. 100).
6. National Center for Education Statistics (1997b, table 136).
7. National Center for Education Statistics (1995, p. 36).

The hard work by students, parents, teachers, and school administrators has to some extent been reflected in higher test scores.

— As measured by the National Assessment of Educational Progress (NAEP), average mathematics and science proficiency for nearly every age and race or ethnic group grew between 1982 and 1994.[8]

— Average Scholastic Assessment Test (SAT) scores in mathematics rose by 19 points between 1980 and 1997.[9] These gains are particularly impressive considering the large increase in the proportion of high school students taking the test.

College enrollment rates have been rising as well. During the 1970s, when the gap in earnings between high school and college graduates was shrinking, enrollment rates stagnated. Later in the decade, when the earnings differential began to widen, the proportion of 18- to 24-year-olds in college expanded as well, a trend that continued throughout the 1980s and 1990s (figure 1-1). The number of associate, bachelor's, and master's degrees awarded increased by about one-third.[10]

The Causes of the Current Financing Crisis

As American families respond to the demands of the labor market, they will need a system of paying for higher education that is up to the task. The current system, however, is showing signs of strain. Tuition at both public and private institutions has increased sharply, while the federal grant and loan programs intended to aid low-income youth have failed to keep pace. Reflecting this breakdown in the financing structure, the already troubling gaps in college entry by race and parental income seem to have widened. Although middle- and higher-income youth seem to be responding to the changing labor market conditions by enrolling in college in greater numbers, low-income youth seem to be lagging. Unfortunately, the next fifteen years will offer little respite as demographic forces increase the pressure on higher education budgets with a rebound in the number of college-age youth of all income levels.

8. National Center for Education Statistics (1997a, pp. 86, 88).

9. These SAT scores are on the new, recentered scale. National Center for Education Statistics (1997b, table 129).

10. This increase in degrees earned is particularly noteworthy given the decrease in the size of the college-age cohort during the period. National Center for Education Statistics (1997b, table 244).

Figure 1-1. *College Enrollment Rates for 18- to 24-Year-Olds and Ratio of Earnings of College Graduates to Earnings of High School Graduates, 1970–94*

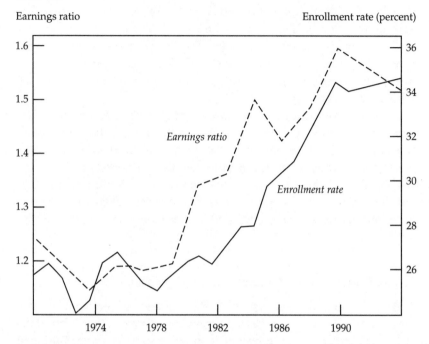

Earnings ratio   Enrollment rate (percent)

Sources: Earnings ratios are from the National Center for Education Statistics (1997a, p. 120). College enrollments were estimated from October Current Population Survey data in National Center for Education Statistics (1997b, table 186, p. 196).

Despite the public's urge to find a scapegoat, the primary cause of rising tuition is not the lazy college professor nor the ineffective college administrator nor the stone-hearted politician. Rather, the current crisis is the result of national economic and demographic forces that are likely to continue.

First, because the labor market value of a college education has sky-rocketed, an increasing proportion of high school students want to invest in further education. The continued rise in the relative earnings of college graduates has been particularly remarkable given this rapid expansion in enrollment. The laws of supply and demand typically dictate that the prices that suddenly go up eventually come down when the market has a chance to react. As employees, high school graduates have become increasingly inexpensive relative to college graduates. As a result, employers have been given a powerful incentive to adjust their hiring policies and to find new ways to employ these less expensive workers. Yet, despite the higher relative cost of more educated workers, the relative earnings premium enjoyed by more educated workers has remained high. One can only infer that the increase in labor market demand is continuing to outpace the supply.[11]

In the face of expanding public college enrollments, state governments have been unable to continue paying the same proportion of the cost for each student, and families have had to make up the difference with higher tuition. In 1980 state and local appropriations covered 83 percent of the educational cost per student at public two-year institutions and 76 percent at four-year institutions. Because parents were paying such a small share of the costs in 1980, even a modest shift of a few percentage points in the burden carried by students and their families meant a large percentage increase in tuition. Even though the share of costs covered by state appropriations fell by only 9 percentage points at public two-year colleges and 14 percentage points at public four-year institutions, the offsetting rise in the portion covered by tuition revenues (that is, gross tuition less the value of scholarships and fellowships) meant that the share paid by students and their families rose by nearly 60 percent.[12]

In other words, the increasing expenses of the colleges were not the sole cause of the rising tuitions at public institutions. Rather, states simply were compelled by other demands on their budgets to cut their subsidies and raise tuitions. Even if the college presidents had been successful in keeping expenditures per pupil in line with inflation, they would have shaved off only one-third of the increases experienced in the past fifteen years.

The federal government, with budgetary concerns of its own, has been unable to fill the financial need created by the higher tuitions at public institutions. The result is that low-income students, who are particularly price sensitive, seem to be losing out. From 1982 to 1992 the

11. Katz and Murphy (1992).

12. Author's tabulation of the Higher Education General Information Survey—Integrated Postsecondary Education Data System database; for more details on categories of cost included in this calculation, see chapter 3. As described by Clotfelter (1996), cost increases seem to have been more important at private institutions. However, public institutions enroll 75 percent of students in higher education.

expansion of college enrollment was greater for those with family incomes above $20,000. There is some evidence that the widening gap is related to rising tuitions in public colleges, since the gap between high- and low-income youth increased more in states with the most rapid public tuition increases.[13] The gap is particularly noteworthy given that a college education has a greater payoff now than in the past four decades.

The pressure on federal and state governments to spend more on higher education is likely to get stronger. The college-age population declined by 11 percent between 1975 and 1995, relieving some of the pressure on costs created by rising enrollment rates. But that population is projected to increase more than 20 percent in the next fifteen years.[14] And the increase is expected to be even more extreme in just a handful of states, notably California.[15]

Thus although labor market trends seem to justify sending more people to college, a college education has become a very expensive undertaking. Even though the tuition at the average public four-year institution is now about $3,000, the actual average expenditure per student is closer to $11,000 a year.[16] Federal and state subsidies for higher education are being stretched thin, and families are being asked to pay a larger share of the costs.

The Focus of This Book

Given that the challenges of the coming decade are likely to require an agenda more ambitious than the incremental reforms of the past decade, the goal of this book is not to provide a detailed diagnosis of any one program but to provide a broad perspective on how the financial aid system works, identify its strengths and structural weaknesses, and offer a rough sketch of possible reforms. To prepare the ground for such a discussion, the book opens with a primer on higher education finance policy in the United States.

Despite minor changes in definitions of eligibility and sources of funding, the same structure has been in place since the mid-1970s. It comprises two basic forms of aid: means-tested grant and loan pro-

13. For more on this, see Kane (1995).
14. Bureau of the Census (1995, table 17).
15. Callan and Finney (1993).
16. National Center for Education Statistics (1997b, table 342).

grams (primarily funded by the federal government) and large operating subsidies to public colleges (provided primarily by state and local governments). Each form of aid has its strengths and weaknesses. The means-tested programs target aid according to an assessment of parents' and their children's income and assets in the previous year. Families submit an application for financial aid and college financial aid counselors respond with a package of grants, loans, and work-study arrangements.

The strength of the current system of means-tested aid, in which eligibility is a function of a long list of family characteristics and students are informed of their eligibility by individual colleges, is that it allows financial aid officers to offer individually tailored packages. Yet an underemphasized weakness of such a system is the uncertainty inevitably created for those who are unfamiliar with aid programs or baffled by financial aid forms. Many families are likely to be unaware of the precise amount of federal aid that is available until they are notified of the amount of the package. To the extent that there is more aid on offer than many families realize or that families are discouraged by the application process, much of the beneficial effect of means-tested aid in opening the doors to college may be blunted.

In contrast, the operating subsidies that allow public institutions to keep tuition low across the board do not require families to fill out a complicated financial aid form in order to benefit. A tuition announcement reported in the local newspaper helps many families anticipate what they can expect to pay for college. Moreover, to the extent that these operating subsidies are paid for with the revenues from broad-based state income taxes, they do not require the same high marginal tax rates on a single year of students' and parents' resources that are implicit in the means-tested aid programs. But this low-tuition, high-subsidy strategy also has disadvantages. When a person's eligibility for such public largesse depends solely on the ability to be admitted to college, the subsidies are bound to benefit higher-income youth disproportionately because they are more likely to have the academic preparation in high school to succeed in college. Indeed, because of the differences in college attendance rates by family income and differences in the number of years of college that high- and low-income youth complete, I estimate that the average high school graduate from a family with income greater than $90,000 a year in 1992–93 could expect to receive about twice the higher-education subsidy from federal, state, and local government of the youth from a family with income less than $20,000, even after counting means-tested aid.

After describing the basic architecture of the financial aid system, the book evaluates the likely causes of the decline in state support (and increase in tuition) at public institutions and the increase in expenditures per student at public and private institutions during the 1980s and 1990s. In the recent furor on Capitol Hill over rising college costs, federal financial aid has been a prime suspect. Although the National Commission on the Cost of Higher Education recently seemed to exonerate federal financial aid policy in placing the blame for increased college costs, the analysis in chapter 3 suggests that federal policy may very well have played an indirect role in the shift in state policy by subsidizing the states that raised public tuition during the 1980s.

Simply plotting the trends in federal student aid expenditures and tuition increases can be a misleading exercise because both could have been driven by some third factor such as a dramatic rise in the costs faced by colleges and universities. Rather, one must study the incentives implicit in the federal financial aid rules and ask whether they would have encouraged a college to raise its tuition or discouraged parents from fighting any such increase more vehemently by providing a subsidy to make up for the loss. According to the analysis in chapter 3, federal financial aid rules did offer substantial subsidies for tuition increases, but only for institutions with tuition below the federal loan and grant limits. This was particularly true in the early 1980s when the federal grant and loan limits were higher and the subsidies larger. The availability of these federal subsidies, particularly when combined with pressures on state legislatures to pay for ballooning state medicaid expenses, may have encouraged states to raise tuition at low-tuition public institutions and cut the share of costs covered by state appropriations. For example, for a middle-class family borrowing less than the Stafford Loan limits, the federal government's payment of interest on a student's loan for four years of college represents a 26 percentage point cut in the cost of the first year and a 16 percentage point cut in the cost of four years of college (at the end of four years, assuming an 8 percent discount rate). With the addition of the Hope Scholarship and Lifetime Learning tax credits in 1997, the federal government now subsidizes 87 percent of the cost over a four-year college career of any tuition increase for middle-class students attending an institution charging less than $1,000 in tuition. As such, federal policy serves as a system of block grants for state residents, essentially encouraging low-tuition states to raise tuition and be reimbursed by federal subsidies.

But while federal financial aid policy may have encouraged increases in public college *tuition*, there is less reason to believe that aid rules have helped drive the increase in *costs* at public or private institutions. Private institutions, where the increase in educational expenditures per student has been enormous, were already generally charging tuitions far beyond the federal limits for grants and loans. In other words, at the price levels where private institutions and their students were bargaining and where the cost (as opposed to tuition) increases were the most pronounced, federal financial aid was largely irrelevant. An extra dollar in tuition when a student already is being charged more than $5,000 generally brings no additional federal subsidy. Even at public institutions the costs per student generally exceeded $5,000. Therefore, although federal financial aid policies may have encouraged changes in state tuition policy at public institutions, there is much less reason to believe that aid was to blame in driving the increases in expenditures at public or private institutions.

So what was behind the higher costs? At public institutions there does not seem to be much to explain. The increase in expenditures per student was comparable in magnitude to the increase in faculty salaries, these institutions' largest expense. But the increase in faculty salaries simply mirrored the increase in the salaries of other similarly educated workers in the 1980s. Universities were competing in the same labor market that was driving up the salaries of the most highly trained workers. In fact, there is some evidence that public institutions responded to increasing salaries in a cost-conscious way by reducing the number of faculty per student.

However, at private institutions the magnitude of the increase in costs remains a mystery. In response to rising faculty salaries, many of the institutions hired more faculty per student, not fewer. As a result, expenditures per student rose even faster than faculty salaries. Although such behavior does not seem consistent with cost consciousness, the demand for the sort of education provided by elite private institutions may simply have grown at the beginning of the 1980s and even more by the early 1990s.

The book then turns to take stock of the progress over the past three decades in providing widespread access to higher education. The debate over the availability of financial aid has traditionally lacked measurable goals. Although all participants pay homage to "access" to higher education and "choice" among institutions, few seem to agree on just how much access is enough. This partly explains why the debate on higher education has become bogged down in the minutiae of the formula for calculating student need or the fees received by private banks. In the 1998 reauthorization of the Higher Education Act, the magnitude of student loan interest rates was the primary object of attention. It is hardly surprising that there is no sense of alarm because there have been no reasonable goals put forward for measuring progress.

Stated simply, the most basic goal of federal and state financial aid should be to ensure that lack of money is not the primary obstacle preventing low-income youth from making crucial educational investments. But several pieces of evidence suggest that ability to pay still weighs heavily in decisions to enroll in college. First, there are gaps in college entry rates between students from poor families and those from wealthier ones even when the young people have similar test scores and similar high school performance. Although the differences are largest for those with test scores in the bottom fourth of their high school class, differences remain even among those with scores in the top fourth. Given the differences in academic preparation of high school graduates, it would be both futile and economically inefficient to use financial aid policy to equalize college entry for rich and poor. Reforming elementary and secondary education is a better way to deal with deficits in academic preparation. However, it is troubling to note that large differences in college entry by family income remain, even among those students who leave high school equally well prepared.

A second piece of evidence suggesting that ability to pay still matters is that families overreact to changes in the price of college and underreact to changes in the return. Dollar for dollar, youth seem to be much more responsive to increased tuition and other expenses than to bigger payoffs. Studies have estimated that a $1,000 difference in tuition is associated with about a 5 percentage point difference in college enrollment.[17] By such an estimate a $1,500 reduction in tuition would thus increase enrollments by 8 percentage points, about as much as enrollments expanded during the 1980s. However, the increase in the payoff

17. Leslie and Brinkman (1988).

for a college education during the 1980s was much larger than $1,500. Even discounting future earnings at the very high rate of 12 percent a year, from 1980 to 1992 the value of future earnings differentials would have grown by $40,000 between high school graduates and those earning college degrees and $24,000 between high school graduates and those completing only some college.

Sources of Financing Constraints

The sources of constraints on financing a college education are unclear, particularly considering the federal grant and loan programs available to low-income students. But rather than raising the borrowing limits or lowering the interest rates charged on federal loans, reducing the nonmonetary costs of negotiating the labyrinthine financial aid system seems a less costly and more promising place to start.

Indeed, the difficulty of applying for financial aid may explain a long-standing puzzle in research on higher education. Most research that has compared college enrollment rates in high- and low-tuition states has found that, all else equal, states with high tuition for public colleges and universities tend to have lower enrollment rates. This is particularly true for enrollments of low-income young people. But there is surprisingly little evidence of any disproportionate increase in college enrollment among low-income youth between the early and late 1970s when many federal loan and grant programs were expanded.[18] (The primary federal means-tested grant program, originally named the Basic Educational Opportunity Grants and later the Pell Grant program, was established in 1973.) The explanation of the paradox may lie in the fact that low-income students, undecided about entering college, *know* about public tuition levels—they can hear about them on television or read about them in newspaper reports—but they may be less able to anticipate how much aid they could receive or to clear all the bureaucratic hurdles on the way to receiving it. Therefore, although the federal government dispenses over $6 billion in Pell Grants each year, it is not at all clear what portion of these students would have been enrolled anyway.

---

18. For more on this issue, see Kane (1994, 1995); Hansen (1983); and McPherson and Schapiro (1991a).

Justifying a Change of Course

The case for public subsidies for higher education has traditionally relied on two economic arguments. The most commonly cited justification emphasizes the hard-to-measure social benefits associated with higher education—improvements in the ability to participate in public debates, greater tolerance between groups, and so forth—that are enjoyed by society as a whole and not just by the students. To the extent that families pay the full cost of education themselves, they are likely to ignore these larger social benefits and may underinvest without some publicly provided inducements. Second, private capital markets are likely to underinvest in education because students lacking other forms of collateral cannot borrow against their future earnings, even for investments that are worthwhile. This is the familiar justification for government loan guarantees as a way to ensure loan financing for worthwhile private investments.

Although education policy has become a popular political touchstone in recent years, with politicians in both parties competing to find new resources for educational initiatives, most proposals lack a coherent rationale justifying greater public involvement in higher education. Advocates typically refer to the need to maintain national economic competitiveness or point to the rising labor market value placed on educational attainment. Yet neither of these observations suggest a need for greater *public* involvement in education beyond ensuring that loan guarantees are sufficient. It is not obvious that the increase in the private returns to college that are driven by labor market changes would have been accompanied by an increase in the other social benefits of higher education. By the traditional arguments for higher education subsidies, the argument for redoubled efforts or a change in direction seems tenuous.

Therefore, in attempting to make the case for a change of course in higher education finance, I rely on a third rationale for public subsidies: differential access to information about applying to college and about the rigors of college life is likely to lead some students to underinvest in their education. And because the payoff from schooling has increased the "cost" of this failure to invest, the cost of this lack of familiarity with college has also increased. Low-income students may always have underinvested in higher education, but during the 1980s and 1990s the economic costs and unfortunate social consequences of that under-investment became more harsh.

For many young people, the first year in college is an experiment in which they are challenged to determine if they are "college material."[19] Some youth simply have better information about how to apply to college and what will be expected of them there. Those with poor information may experiment too little. Of course, the most direct way to address any underinvestment resulting from this lack of familiarity would be to improve access to information about applying for federal financial aid or to simplify the application process.

But that is not the only way to lower the costs of experimenting with college. For instance, student financial aid dollars ought to be distributed so that the incremental gain in educational attainment (or, more accurately, in the public good generated by educational attainment) for each dollar of financial aid given college freshmen equals the incremental gain for each dollar of financial aid for college seniors. Yet when college freshmen are more likely than college seniors to have their decisions changed by an extra dollar in aid, there are potential gains to be had from raising the amount of aid available to a college freshmen to an amount greater than the aid available to a college senior. For instance, rather than providing grants to students for all four years in college, the same funds could be used to offer larger grants to students in their first two years of college, essentially encouraging those who are uncertain of their college prospects to learn about their college potential by enrolling. Those who discover the benefits of a college training could then be expected to borrow a larger share of the costs during their final years of college.

Whether a student is entering the first or the third year of college, a dollar of aid that encourages someone to attend an extra year results in an extra year of education. However, encouraging someone to try their first year of college also creates an option value with the possibility that the student will learn to thrive there.

There is some evidence that the threshhold from high school to college is more difficult to cross than the subsequent transitions from the first to the second, second to third, and third to fourth years of college.

Figure 1-2 uses information on the educational attainment of 25- to 35-year-old men in the 1990–91 Current Population Survey (March

19. Manski (1989) uses this analogy to understand college dropouts.

Figure 1-2. *School Continuation and Average Hourly Earnings,*
by Highest Grade Completed

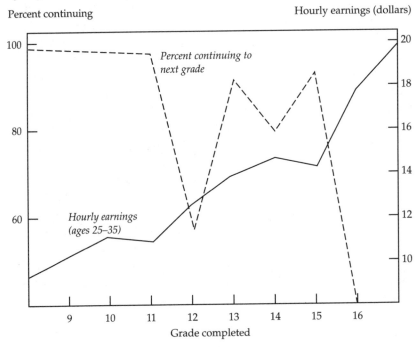

Percent continuing   Hourly earnings (dollars)

Source: Author's tabulations of 1990–91 Current Population Survey.

supplement) to estimate the proportion of young people completing
each grade level that choose to go on to the next grade level.[20] More
than 95 percent of those who reported completing eighth grade entered
ninth grade. A similarly large share of those who reported completing
the ninth through eleventh grades reported continuing to the next
grade level. But less than 60 percent of those completing twelfth grade
reported going on to attend even one year of college. And there is a
similar falloff in continuation rates between college graduation and
graduate school. The proportion of youth going on to the next grade

20. The data from 1990–91 are used because these are the last two years that respondents were asked to report single years of schooling attended. Beginning in 1992 there has
been no way to distinguish those completing one, two, or three years of college with no
degree.

level falls at those points where students cross from one institution into another, even though the payoffs rise smoothly. Our goal should be to lower the thresholds at these transitions.

Meanwhile, figure 1-2 also shows that average hourly earnings per year of schooling completed increase more smoothly. There is no apparent fall in the increment in earnings associated with completing a year of college relative to the other increments. With the payoff to education appearing to increase so smoothly, the sudden drop-off in school continuation between high school and college seems puzzling.

Those who study high school dropout behavior know that the transition from middle school to junior high school can be extremely important. But at the boundary between high school and college, students not only have to find their way in a very different institutional environment, they also suddenly have to start paying tuition.

The proportion of those completing the first year of college who go on to attend a second year is closer to the continuation rates of high school students. Therefore, the limiting factor in school continuation does not seem to be tuition payments alone, because students considering their second year in college generally face the same incremental tuition costs as those considering the first year in college. Rather, something about the change in institutional setting seems to result in significant numbers of students falling off track.

Beyond front-loading eligibility for federal grant programs to those in their first years of college, there are a number of ways to avoid these problems. The first is to make simplicity and transparency fundamental to the aid application process. Families' uncertainty about the availability and potential amount of aid is, in part, a *result of* the design of federal financial aid policy. Currently, the marketing of federal financial aid is done largely by college financial aid offices when they offer aid packages to the students who apply for help. One strength of such a system is that the mixture of grants, loans, and work-study can be tailored to meet the particular needs of each student. However, parents and students are usually uncertain about the extent of aid available right up to the time they receive their package, when it is too late to adjust their savings decisions or to expand the range of colleges to which they have applied. And those whose decisions we would most hope to affect, those who would not be going to college in the absence of aid, are probably least likely to be able to navigate the system easily and anticipate the amount of aid available.

The U.S. Department of Education has tried many times to simplify the federal financial aid application process. But merely rearranging and reformatting a complicated list of questions contribute little. The price of real transparency may be to shorten the list of factors included in the need-analysis formula itself—for instance, basing expected family contributions to college education solely on family size and income. My calculations suggest that one could capture two-thirds of the variation in expected family contributions knowing these two characteristics. A simple table could replace the federal need-analysis system. Any loss in the targeting of benefits (some particularly high-asset, low-income young people would benefit and some moderate-income, low-asset families would lose) must be considered relative to the gain in transparency.

Second, the U.S. Department of Education should conduct randomized controlled experiments designed to evaluate the effectiveness of different forms of aid in affecting student choices. It seems reasonable to believe that an extra dollar in grant aid is more effective than an extra dollar of student loans in encouraging young people to experiment with college. However, a dollar in grants is a much more expensive way for taxpayers to solve a family's short-term liquidity problem than a dollar in loans. (In fact, using congressional cost estimates, the cost of a dollar in grants is roughly six times as large as the cost of a dollar in loans. Although the actual subsidy depends on future trends in interest rates, my calculations suggest that a dollar in grant aid costs between three and six times as much.) Yet the department has no way to weigh the bang for the buck achieved by these different policy instruments.

Given the magnitude of the public investments at stake in federal and state student aid policy, this is a gap worth filling. For instance, in the past two decades policymakers have sponsored numerous experimental evaluations of the employment and training programs for welfare recipients and, more recently, for the job training programs funded under the Department of Labor. However, the dollars at stake in these programs are small when compared to the size of public subsidies for higher education: federal spending on employment and training programs for welfare recipients was roughly $1 billion a year following the Family Support Act of 1988; appropriations under the Job Training Partnership Act (JTPA) were less than $2 billion in the early 1990s at the time of the JTPA evaluation. In contrast, the Pell Grant program alone costs more than $6 billion a year, states and local government spend another $49 billion in direct subsidies to public institutions, and about

$33 billion of federally guaranteed educational loans are originated each year.[21] Given the magnitude of the public investment, an evaluation of the relative effects of different types of aid is long overdue. The Department of Education should fund an experimental evaluation of its student aid programs, incorporating the menu of policy options facing policymakers (grants, loans, better high school counseling for students considering college), and estimate the impact of each of these types of policies on college-going rates of different types of youth. Only with such estimates in hand could we begin to have a more productive debate over how to achieve the goal of equalizing college entry among equally prepared students.

Third, policymakers should think creatively about ways to target benefits other than through the current system for analyzing need. Until recently, few policymakers have taken the tax rates implicit in the need-analysis formula very seriously. At a time when most students attended low-tuition public institutions, this may have been appropriate, because a majority of students would have had income and assets that placed them beyond the range of financial eligibility and therefore beyond the range where implicit taxes from the student aid formula mattered. However, if public tuition continues to rise, an increasing number of middle-income families may become eligible for such aid and the number of youth subject to such taxes will rise. Rather than continue to base public subsidies solely on a means test that evaluates parents' and students' resources at college entry, a larger share of the subsidy could be tied to the future income of students through forgiving some part of the loan if the former student earns a relatively low income.

There is some history of targeting aid based upon what students do after college. For instance, in the fall of 1998, the reauthorized Higher Education Act provided loan forgiveness of up to $5,000 for new teachers working in certain low-income schools. Moreover, the Taxpayer Relief Act of 1997 ensured that student loans provided by tax-exempt organizations (such as private not-for-profit or public colleges) can now be forgiven with no additional tax liability for the borrower, as long as the person is working for government or a nonprofit institution in an underserved area or occupation. Other approaches would be to make the income-contingent repayment plan currently available to student

21. For the Pell Grant program, see College Board (1998, table 7).

borrowers more generous or provide a tax credit to those whose loan payments exceed some portion of their income in a given year. (The latter proposal might even be paid for by converting the difficult-to-administer Hope Scholarship or Lifetime Learning tax expenditures into an income-contingent tax credit for student borrowers.)

Forward-looking means testing has several advantages. First, it offers "insurance" to all families, high and low income, concerned whether their children will be able to shoulder student debt. The average difference in earnings between those with and without a college degree has widened, but the variability in students' gains from college also seems to have increased. Although there may be little justification for greater government involvement arising from an increase in the average financial returns to schooling, government may have a legitimate role in providing some insurance against the greater uncertainty surrounding a student's possible range of future earnings. Parents and students may value this additional peace of mind even if they never actually have to sign up for the income-contingent repayment option.

Forward-looking means testing does not involve the same difficulty in distinguishing dependent students, those whose parents' resources are considered in the determination of need, from independent students. The distinction becomes moot if subsidies are disbursed on the basis of students' subsequent income rather than prior income and savings. And because it treats younger and older college entrants similarly, forward-looking means testing may be better suited to serve the goal of lifelong learning as older workers seek to upgrade their skills.

Forward-looking means testing can also greatly diminish the marginal tax rates on income and savings implicit in financial aid formulas. Basing eligibility for a given subsidy on a lifetime of earnings can allow for lower implicit tax rates than if a single year of income and assets are used.

Finally, moving a larger share of the subsidies from backward- to forward-looking means testing would remove part of the uncertainty surrounding the decision to enter college and move it to the years after college. The financial aid system would be simplified: students would see the same federal loan dollars on offer to be paid off later on the basis of income. As such, they could make decisions about whether to invest in college without first having to decide how much money they would have to provide out of their own pockets.

The biggest challenge in the design of income-contingent loan forgiveness programs in the past has been overcoming the problem of adverse selection in self-financing plans.[22] This proposal differs in that it would divert other funds—such as from the in-school interest subsidy or other educational tax credits—to fund the loan forgiveness.

Conclusion

A dollar in federal subsidy that does not lead to a change in behavior leaves the nation no better prepared than before to respond to the demands of the new labor market. Much of the current public subsidy to higher education seems directed at those who would have attended college anyway. For instance, the estimate of tuition effects on enrollment rates reported later suggests that a $1,000 across-the-board subsidy to those attending public institutions would yield roughly a 5 percentage point increase in the proportion of high school graduates entering college within twenty months after high school. In other words, a $1,000 across-the-board tuition cut for all 8 million full-time-equivalent students enrolled in public institutions of higher education would yield a 5 percentage point increase in college attendance for the 2.6 million new high school graduates in a given year, implying a cost of more than $61,000 for each new college entrant. The cost per incremental student is likely to be much higher for across-the-board subsidies than for more targeted programs. The policy recommendations in this book are intended to generate more leverage with existing resources in allowing students to respond to the increased value of education by enrolling in college.

A college is in effect a refinery where the ore of raw intelligence is transformed into the sharp-edged metal of technical skill and abstract insight. As the price of metal increases, the material with the highest ore content increases in value the most. But so too does the value of all grades of ore. Limiting college enrollment or protecting the standards of admission into college is counterproductive: the economy is demanding that we process more, not less. And although this may imply a decline in the average academic preparation of the students, we should not be erecting barriers to the neediest among them. Improving the quality of elementary and secondary education is only one way to invest. It may not even be the way most likely to yield results. This book is about another way: investing in the quantity of schooling received by better targeting public subsidies in higher education.

22. Krueger and Bowen (1993).

2

How We Pay for College

When budgets strained under the weight of soaring health care costs during the early 1990s, the Clinton administration led the American public in a crash course of talk show debates and town hall discussions to explain the afflictions of the nation's health care finance system. Today, the system for financing higher education is at least as mysterious for most Americans as the health care system was a decade ago. True, families have been well aware of inflating tuition bills. But tuition is only the most visible cost (revenue from tuition and fees covered only one-third of the $144 billion in educational expenditures by colleges in 1994–95).[1] Just as in health care, families are paying for college in many more ways than they realize: as taxpayers, students, and parents. This chapter describes in some detail the system for financing higher education.

The Components of the Financing System

At the risk of oversimplifying, six components work together to finance the education of the 15 million students enrolled in college each year.[2] First, state and local governments provide $49 billion in annual operating subsidies to public institutions. This subsidy is eight times larger than the largest federal grant program for low-income students and considerably more than total borrowing under the federal loan programs. Because the subsidies are mostly invisible, the true cost of a college education is not clear to taxpayers, and college administrators are relieved of the need to justify the costs to parents. No application forms

1. National Center for Education Statistics (1997b, tables 324, 334).
2. National Center for Education Statistics (1998, table 329).

need to be filled out for these indirect tuition subsidies. They are generally not means tested. Yet they have been an essential source of funding for many students.

Means-tested government grant and loan programs are the second major source of financing for higher education. These subsidies are based on an assessment of a student's and, for a dependent student, his or her parents' income and assets at the time of enrollment. Thus ability to pay is determined by a backward-looking assessment of parents' previous year's income and assets, as opposed to a forward-looking assessment of the students' earnings later in life. Although all states operate their own means-tested programs, the federal government provides the lion's share of such aid, primarily through the Pell Grant program, federal work-study program, and federal loan programs. Spending on federal grant and work-study programs totaled $7.8 billion in 1997–98. The federal government also guaranteed $33 billion in new loans for college in that period, including $3 billion in loans to parents of college students. In contrast, state spending on grant programs totaled $3.3 billion.[3] State aid for college education is still primarily in the form of operating support for the colleges themselves, keeping tuition low for in-state students rather than targeting aid to individuals. Less than 10 percent of state spending on higher education is provided through means-tested financial aid programs.

Colleges also distribute their own aid to students. They provide price discounts based on academic and athletic talent and financial need. These institutional grants or tuition discounts amounted to $11 billion in the 1997–98 school year.[4] Forty-three percent of full-time students at private four-year colleges receive some institutional grant aid. But the aid is primarily a phenomenon at private institutions: only 11 percent of full-time students at public colleges were receiving any grant aid from institutional funds in 1992–93.[5]

Using resources provided by the federal campus-based aid programs, schools also enjoy some discretion in distributing their allocations of certain federal grants, work-study funds, and specially subsidized loans. In 1997–98 they distributed almost $2.6 billion through such programs as

3. College Board (1998, table 2).

4. College Board (1998, table 2).

5. Author's calculations based on the National Postsecondary Student Aid Study, 1992–93.

Supplemental Educational Opportunity Grants (SEOGs), the Perkins Loan program, and federal work-study programs.[6]

Universities can also draw on endowment income to pay expenses. In 1994–95, endowment income accounted for 5 percent of current-fund revenues at private institutions but less than 1 percent at public institutions.[7] Endowments, however, are important at only a few colleges: in 1995, ten institutions controlled more than a quarter of total endowment wealth in higher education.[8]

The Taxpayer Relief Act of 1997 created a number of new federal tax expenditures for higher education. The package of tax credits and tax deductions has been estimated to cost $39 billion in the first five years, making it slightly larger than the Pell Grant program, the primary federal grant program for low-income youth.[9]

Finally, students and families themselves financed a large portion of the cost of college out of family income and savings. In millions of individual agreements hashed out over dinner tables around the country, they agreed to pay for much of the direct costs of higher education out of their own pockets.

The long arm of federal policy is not absent from these dinner table sessions. A federal formula explicitly determines "financial need" and an "expected family contribution" for those who do not meet the definition of independent students. Dependent students are prevented from receiving any subsidized federal loan or grant aid in excess of their financial need. If a student's parents are not willing to contribute the amount suggested by the need analysis, the student must find other sources to bridge the gap. Therefore, the federal governments' expected family contribution becomes a self-fulfilling prophecy if students have few other alternatives.

Determining "Expected Family Contribution" and "Financial Need"

Each spring, millions of students and their parents fill out the Free Application for Federal Student Aid (FAFSA) and submit it to a federal

6. College Board (1998, table 2).
7. National Center for Education Statistics (1997b, tables 325, 326).
8. National Center for Education Statistics (1997b, table 352).
9. U.S. House of Representatives (1997, pp. 776–78).

contractor for processing (the U.S. Department of Education pays the cost of the processing). The current version of the application contains 108 items, including detailed questions on the income and assets of students, their spouses, and their parents. In many ways the application is like a tax form, probing for information on family income from various sources, family savings, and household composition. However, there is one very important difference: there is no bottom-line calculation on the financial aid application. Instead, students and their parents must submit the form and wait to be told what their "expected family contribution" is. Naturally, given the mysterious nature of the "need-analysis" machinations, this process generates a certain amount of anxiety.

But although it may be well hidden, the formula underlying the need analysis is not very difficult to understand. Dependent students must report their own income and the income and assets of their parents. The definition of dependency was clarified in 1992: only those older than age 24, veterans, married students, graduate students, orphans, or those who have children of their own are considered independent and therefore exempt from reporting parental income and assets. The number of years a student has been filing his or her own tax return, the size of past parental financial support, and other factors more easily subject to manipulation are no longer relevant.

In the calculation of parents' expected contribution, "available" income is defined using their adjusted gross income from their federal tax form in the most recently completed calendar year. Untaxed income such as social security income and before-tax contributions to IRA or 401(k) plans is added to adjusted gross income. Certain allowable expenses such as employees' social security tax payments; federal, state, and local income tax; and an employment allowance of up to $2,800 for two-earner families and single-parent families are subtracted. Depending on their family size and number of students in college, parents are allowed to protect a certain amount of income. For the 1999–2000 school year, a family of four with one student in college was allowed $18,850 in after-tax income before being expected to contribute anything toward their child's college education.

A portion of a family's assets is also considered available to the student for financing college.[10] But because of recent changes in the formula,

10. Between 1993 and 1998, those with family incomes of less than $50,000 who filed a 1040A or 1040EZ tax form did not face the asset test. The asset test was restored in 1998.

assets are increasingly irrelevant for federal aid programs. Future pension benefits and IRA and 401(k) account balances have always been excluded from consideration. Although many private colleges continue to use housing assets in distributing their own financial aid awards, they were excluded in calculating eligibility for federal aid programs in 1993. For federal aid, relevant assets include only cash and business assets and investments that are not acquired through retirement accounts. Families are allowed to "protect" assets below certain limits that vary by parents' age and the number of adults in the household. For instance, in 1999–2000 two-parent families with the oldest parent aged 45 could have as much as $42,500 in cash, savings, or other nonretirement, nonhousing assets before the assets are considered by the federal need analysis.[11]

Any family income above the income protection limit and 12 percent of any countable assets above the asset protection limit are then considered available for financing the dependent student's education. The schedule is progressive; marginal rates range from 22 percent for the first $11,000 to 47 percent of any amounts exceeding $22,100. Table 2-1 shows the expected parental contributions for families of four, with one earner and one child in college. For instance, middle-class parents with an income of $50,000 and cash assets of $25,000 would be expected to provide $4,759 each year toward the expenses of a child in college.

The income and assets of students, whether they are dependent or independent, are implicitly taxed more heavily by the federal financial aid formula. Dependent students are allowed to protect up to $2,200 in their own and their spouses' income after paying federal, state, and social security taxes. Above $2,200, a student loses $.50 in aid eligibility for every $1.00 in income. And 35 percent of any savings—there is no asset protection for the student—is also expected to be available to pay the cost of college.

Federal Financial Aid Programs

Federal financial aid comes in three forms: grants, wage subsidies, and loans. Unlike loans and wage subsidies, grant aid need not be paid

11. If a student's parents are divorced, the income and assets of only the custodial parent are considered. If the custodial parent has remarried, the income and assets of the stepparent are also considered in the federal formula. Just as many colleges consider home equity in distributing their own aid, some institutions consider the resources of both parents in making institutional aid awards.

Table 2-1. *Expected Parental Annual Contribution in Calculating*
Federal Financial Aid for Higher Education, 1996–97 [a]

Current dollars

Parents' before-tax income	Net assets [b]		
	25,000	50,000	100,000
20,000	0	0	1,057
30,000	1,086	1,284	2,629
40,000	2,663	2,888	4,713
50,000	4,759	5,101	7,768
60,000	7,831	8,254	11,074
70,000	10,587	11,010	13,830
80,000	13,574	13,997	16,817
90,000	16,561	16,984	19,804
100,000	18,217	18,640	21,460

Source: Author's calculations.

a. The estimates use the federal methodology to calculate expected parental contribution for a two-parent family of four, assuming that the older parent is 45 and employed, the other parent is not employed, the income is from employment, the family used the standard deduction, the family did not file forms 1040A or 1040EZ, and only one child is enrolled in college. Calculations use 1999–2000 need analysis.

b. Excludes primary residence and family farm.

back and does not require a student to spend valuable study or leisure time (such as required by wage-subsidy programs) to qualify.

By far the largest federal grant program is the Pell Grant program. For most students, Pell Grant eligibility is calculated simply by subtracting one's expected family contribution from the grant maximum at the time. For instance, the maximum for 1998–99 was $3,000. Students with expected family contributions less than $2,800 will qualify for a Pell Grant if they file a federal financial aid application and are attending a qualifying school; students with expected family contributions greater than $2,800 will not qualify (because the minimum Pell Grant is $200). As implied by the expected family contributions shown in table 2-1, these conditions imply that Pell Grant eligibility for dependent students with no income or assets would phase out at family incomes between $30,000 and $40,000.

In most cases Pell Grant eligibility is the same regardless of the cost of the college—whether tuition is $2,000 or $25,000. Officially, a grant is not allowed to exceed the total "cost of attendance." But because cost of attendance includes an allowance for living expenses, few institutions have tuition low enough for a grant to approach the maximum.[12]

In addition to Pell Grants a student may qualify for federally guaranteed student loans. The two primary programs for student borrowers are the "subsidized" and "unsubsidized" Stafford Loan programs. Although both programs are subsidized in the sense that a student would be unlikely to receive similar terms on uncollateralized loans in the private markets, the primary difference between a subsidized and unsubsidized loan is that the federal government pays the interest on the subsidized loans while a student is enrolled in school at least half time. Otherwise, the interest rates and the loan repayment plans are similar. The interest rate for subsidized and unsubsidized loans is variable and calculated as the rate for the ninety-one-day Treasury bill on June 1 of that year plus 2.3 percent. Both are subject to a cap of 8.25 percent.

Dependent students can borrow up to $2,625 during their first year (in combined borrowing under the subsidized and unsubsidized loan programs), $3,500 during the second year, and $5,500 a year during the final two years. However, only those with financial need after counting Pell Grant aid and other financial aid qualify for a subsidized loan. Even those without financial need can borrow under the unsubsidized loan programs, but the borrowing is subjected to the same $2,625, $3,500, and $5,500 limits.

Obviously, these Stafford Loan limits are well below the sticker price at most colleges. But there are other sources of borrowing for some students under the federal programs. Independent students are allowed to borrow an additional $4,000 a year during their first two years in college and $5,000 a year afterward under the unsubsidized Stafford program. Parents of dependent students are also allowed to supplement student borrowing by borrowing up to the full cost of attendance (minus any other aid) under the Parent Loans for Undergraduate Students (PLUS) program.[13] The interest rates are higher on these loans, and payments begin immediately.

12. The insensitivity of Pell Grants to tuition changes has been a matter of debate in recent years. Under current law a student is eligible for only half the difference between $2,700 and the Pell Grant maximum when an institution's tuition is less than $150. However, because the Pell Grant maximum is only $300 above $2,700, this provision has only a small effect on a recipient's award.

13. The variable interest rate on PLUS loans is the fifty-two week Treasury bill rate on June 1 plus 3.1 percent. The variable interest rate on current PLUS loans cannot exceed 9 percent.

The federal government allocates to individual campuses funds that the institution can distribute to students with financial need. These campus-based programs are the remnants of the financial aid system that existed before the Pell Grant program was established in 1973, when financial aid dollars were allocated to specific institutions rather than allowed to follow the students. The three primary campus-based programs are the Perkins Loan program, the federal work-study program, and the Supplemental Educational Opportunity Grant program.

The Perkins program provides loans with the most favorable terms of all the federal programs: a fixed interest rate of 5 percent with an exemption while the student is in school. Participating institutions are authorized to make a limited volume of such loans with federal funds. If designated by a school to be eligible for a Perkins Loan, undergraduate students may be allowed to borrow $3,000 a year up to $15,000. However, in 1992–93, only 10 percent of students receiving federal aid also received a Perkins Loan.

Under the federal work-study program, the federal government provides an allotment to each campus to subsidize up to 75 percent of the wages of students working on campus or community jobs. The jobs must pay at least the federal minimum wage and the funds must be allotted to students with "need," that is, those for whom the cost of attendance minus grant aid minus expected family contribution is positive. The subsidy is actually much larger than 75 percent, given the way work-study income is treated in the formula for computing the family contribution. Although the need analysis imposes a marginal "tax rate" of 50 percent on most student earnings, income earned from work-study is not counted in calculating a family's contribution. Therefore, a work-study job paying $6 an hour is equivalent to any other job paying $12 an hour for a student with an expected family contribution sufficiently low to qualify for grant aid.

Finally, schools can use their allotments of federal campus-based aid to make Supplemental Educational Opportunity Grants of up to $4,000 to students with expected family contributions less than the cost of attendance. The 1997–98 federal appropriation for the program was $583 million.[14]

14. College Board (1998, table 1).

Anomalies in the Financial Aid Formulas

The quickest way to find the weaknesses in the financial aid system is to read one of the many unofficial manuals that have been written for parents preparing to send their children to college. Here are some of the more glaring holes in the system that are pointed out in the manuals.

Having two kids in school at the same time is like a two-for-one sale.[15] Under the federal financial aid formula, a family with two members in college is expected to contribute only half as much per member as a family of equal resources with one person currently attending. This is not a family size adjustment. Elsewhere in the formula, larger families are allowed to protect more income from the "taxation" implied by the formula. Rather, the effect of such a rule is to distribute aid on the basis of the timing of college attendance. Families with children closer in age, or in which a secondary worker has returned to school part time, or in which students stay in school longer and are therefore more likely to overlap are eligible for considerably more aid than other families of equal size.

"The single most effective way to reduce the family contribution is to make line 31 on your 1040 federal income tax return look as small as possible."[16] A parent's and an applicant's income in the most recent completed calendar year is the only income that matters in determining eligibility for financial aid. This necessarily implies very high tax rates on a single year's income for those who are eligible for aid. Because such tax rates apply to income only during the years in which their children are in college, families have a strong incentive to shift income into the years before and after college. Job bonuses and capital gains are likely candidates for shifting. In addition, because aid is based on adjusted gross income, above-the-line deductions to income produce eligibility for greater amounts of aid. The self-employed enjoy an advantage, therefore, because their business expenses are deducted before the calculation of adjusted gross income.[17]

The tax on assets is imposed every year a child is in school, implying high cumulative tax rates on savings. Parental assets above a threshold are in-

15. Drawn from Chany and Martz (1994, p. 36).
16. Chany and Martz (1994, p. 41).
17. Wage and salary workers can deduct unreimbursed work expenses, but this is a "below-the-line" deduction.

cluded in a family's ability to pay for school. For instance, a two-parent family with a head aged 50 years old is allowed to protect $48,400. However, any savings above this amount is subject to a maximum "tax rate" of 5.64 percent. The magnitude of the tax rate on savings is one issue on which the guidebooks for parents often miss the mark by deemphasizing the savings tax. This rate does not sound very high until one recognizes that the same rate is applied for each year that a child is in college. If a family has a child in school for four years, the marginal dollar in savings results in $.23 in reduced financial need over the four years. If a family has two children attending college consecutively for eight years, the tax rate is nearly 50 percent. In other words, every dollar put away for college may be offset by nearly a $.50 decline in estimated need over eight years of college education.[18]

The actual impact of student financial aid rules on family savings is, however, tempered somewhat. First, only parental savings above the asset protection allowance are subject to the financial aid tax. For instance, for the 1999–2000 school year, a two-parent family where the elder parent is 45 years old could have financial assets (excluding home equity and pension savings) of up to $42,500 before having its federal financial aid status affected.

Second, high-income or high-asset families face a zero marginal tax from the federal financial aid system if their income or assets are sufficiently high for students to be ineligible for federal financial aid. Tuition, required fees, and room and board at the average public four-year institution in 1996–97 totaled $7,331.[19] As implied by table 2-1, a two-parent family (with assets of $25,000) with a child attending the average public four-year university in 1996–97 would have faced zero marginal tax on savings or income as long as the family income was above $60,000, since the average expected family contribution exceeded tuition and room and board at those institutions. Three-quarters of college students attend public institutions.[20]

Third, all these inferences regarding implicit tax rates assume that any gap between expected family contribution and the cost of attendance—the student's financial need—is being met. However, not all financial

18. Feldstein (1995).
19. National Center for Education Statistics (1997b, table 312).
20. National Center for Education Statistics (1997b, table 200).

need is met, and as a result the marginal tax rates are often substantially less than the rates implied by the expected family contribution formula. For instance, Andrew Dick and Aaron Edlin estimate that families faced marginal income tax rates between 2 and 16 percent and marginal savings tax rates between 8 and 26 percent as a result of the student financial aid system.[21]

For most families, the implicit tax rates in the financial aid formula are difficult to observe. Nowhere on the Free Application for Federal Student Aid is the expected family contribution formula explained. Rather, families are simply asked to report family income, family size, financial assets, and the other data required for calculating financial aid. Because there is no bottom line, there is no way to evaluate the impact of changes in income, savings, family size, or other items on the calculation. The information is run through the federal formula, and families are informed of their expected family contribution by mail. Although the many privately published financial aid guidebooks attempt to lift the veil of mystery surrounding the expected contribution, many families are likely to be ignorant of the formula. (And even if they learn about the implicit tax rates after seeing their financial aid package change from year to year while their children are in college, it would be too late to have an effect on savings behavior.) Indeed, many families seem to be ignorant of the range of financial aid programs that are available, much less understand the formula that establishes their eligibility.[22]

One way to judge the effects of the financial aid formula on private savings would be to look for evidence of families "stacking up" at the asset protection limits in the financial aid formulas.[23] If families were aware of the formula and were adjusting their assets accordingly to avoid the implicit taxes of the financial aid system, one would expect to

21. Dick and Edlin (1997).

22. Orfield (1992).

23. Using data from the 1986 Survey of Consumer Finances, Martin Feldstein (1995) estimated that the student financial aid formulas discouraged accumulation of $66 billion in assets in 1986. However, because the marginal tax rates are themselves a function of assets, it is a difficult matter to disentangle empirically the effect of marginal tax rates on savings.

Feldstein's approach was to include a quadratic in income to predict family wealth and then use predicted family wealth to calculate the marginal tax rates on savings. Because income is also included in the second stage, this method implicitly uses the nonlinearities in the formula determining marginal tax rates as well as the quadratic income term to

Figure 2-1. *Distribution of Difference between Parents' Reported Net Worth and Asset Protection Allowance among Undergraduates, 1992–93*[a]

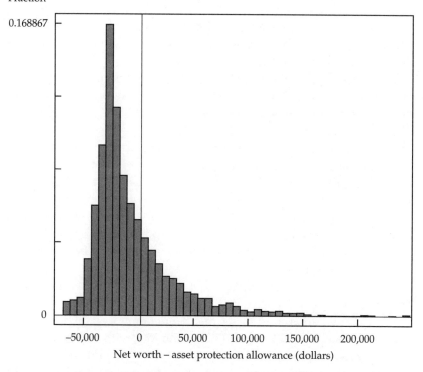

Fraction

Net worth – asset protection allowance (dollars)

Source: Author's calculations based on data from institutional Student Aid Report of National Postsecondary Student Aid Study, 1992–93.

a. Graduate students, independent students, and those with parents reporting nonzero business value were excluded.

see an unusual number of households with assets equal to the asset protection allowance. Figure 2-1 reflects data on parental assets from the National Postsecondary Student Aid Study of 1992–93, the year before the exclusion of home equity came into effect. The data are drawn from the students' student aid reports on file at college financial aid offices,

---

"instrument" for the marginal tax rate while including factors such as income and number of children in the equation. This approach relies heavily on the particular specification of the second stage for identification.

reflecting what families actually reported in their aid applications (rather than their responses to a subsequent questionnaire that they may or may not have filled out consistently).[24] Although each family faces a different asset protection allowance depending on the number of parents in the household and the age of the elder parent, I show the distribution of the difference between families' reported net worth and the asset protection allowance.

First, only a quarter of the sample of dependent undergraduates had parents with assets above the asset protection allowance (although, because high-asset households were probably less likely to apply for aid, this estimate probably understates the proportion of households affected.) Second, and most important, the distribution offers very little evidence that parents are reporting assets close to the asset protection allowances. There is no evidence that parents stack up at the asset protection allowance as would be expected if they were moving their assets around to avoid the tax. As an informal test of the impact of the savings incentives either on the amount of assets reported on the financial aid form, figure 2-1 does not provide strong evidence of a behavioral response to the asset test.[25]

Housing equity has been excluded from the federal formula. Beginning in 1993 housing equity was excluded from the federal formula for calculating financial aid, thus boosting the number of families qualifying for Pell Grants and subsidized Stafford Loans. Families with college-age children now have a strong incentive to move their equity into housing. For instance, families with financial assets above the protected amount could use the resources to prepay a portion of their mortgages and, when their children emerged from college, refinance their homes and reinvest their savings in a mutual fund or some other financial instrument.

On one hand, the impact of financial aid rules on savings behavior is likely to be weaker as a result of the exclusion of home equity because the most alert parents, who would have been willing to adjust their sav-

---

24. To avoid any noise introduced by the valuation of business and farm assets, I excluded those with nonzero business or farm assets.

25. Admittedly, this may not be a test of the full savings impact of the financial aid rules. Even if families do not know exactly where the marginal tax rates become zero, they may understand, however vaguely, that a dollar in savings could hurt them when it comes time to apply for college and adjust their behavior accordingly. But given that marginal tax rates are a function of income and assets, it is difficult to do much better.

ings behavior, can now avoid the tax by shifting resources into home equity. On the other hand, the asset test has now become a tax on naive nonstrategic behavior. From the point of view of economic efficiency, taxing the myopic or the nonstrategic may be desirable because those families who are caught by the tax are those whose savings behavior is the most inflexible. After all, it is the scramble to avoid taxes that produces "inefficiency." However, one might be concerned about the fairness of punishing those less aware of the labyrinthine financial aid system that has been constructed.

Independent or dependent? The financial aid system was not designed with "nontraditional" students in mind. It is the secret hope of many parents to declare their college-age children independent to avoid the "taxation" of parental income and assets in calculating need. However, for college students of the traditional age, the current financial aid formulas no longer allow that loophole. The typical undergraduate college student—one who is younger than age 24, is unmarried, has no dependents, and has not served in the military—has no way to hide parental resources from consideration.

But the same rules designed for the traditional college student do not work very well in determining the need of independent students. First, students taking fewer than six credits of course work do not qualify for student loan programs (although they may qualify for a Pell Grant if they do not yet have a bachelor's degree). This is one reason state and local governments have been under pressure to keep tuition low at community colleges and four-year comprehensive universities: the institutional subsidy is often the only aid that adult students attending less than half time can receive. Less than half-time attendance may be the best option for those who must also hold down a job.

Second, income in the previous calendar year is not likely to be a good indicator of a student's ability to pay, particularly one who is entering a second year of study. The tax rates on students' income are much higher than on parents. Those who have lost their jobs or who plan to switch careers may often not be eligible for much aid during their first year in college because 50 percent of their income and 35 percent of their assets are considered available for college. After having been enrolled in school, however, they can expect to receive considerable aid during their second year if they did not work much during their first.

The Price Students Actually Pay

The mean tuition paid and financial aid received by full-time, dependent undergraduates in 1992–93 is shown in table 2-2. The averages, which include those with no aid, are reported separately by type of college attended. Tuition charges are first reported net of any federal, state, or institutional grant aid. The last two columns show student borrowing. The mean sticker price—tuition and required fees—for full-time students in 1992–93 was $1,200, $2,400, and $11,000 at public two-year, public four-year, and private four-year colleges, respectively. At public two-year and four-year colleges this is a fairly good indicator of the direct cost of college for those families with incomes of $60,000 or more. Young people from these families qualify for very little federal student aid, and public institutions have very little institutional aid to offer their students. Fewer than one out of six dependent undergraduates with family incomes greater than $60,000 received any form of grant aid at public institutions.

However, for low-income students or even for many of those from high-income families who are attending private institutions, there is often some form of grant aid available. The aid is typically sufficient to cover the full cost of tuition for students from families with incomes less than $20,000 at public two-year and four-year institutions. However, private institutions typically do not provide sufficient grant aid to cover tuition costs for low-income students. As a result, even the lowest-income students typically borrowed to help pay their tuition bills at private institutions. The average student with a family income below $20,000 (including those with no loans) borrowed $2,400 a year to help pay for private college during the 1992–93 school year (table 2-2).

Federal and state grant aid is targeted primarily on students with family incomes below $20,000 and is largely phased out for those with incomes between $20,000 and $50,000. Very few with family incomes above $50,000 receive any federal or state grant aid.

Room and Board Charges Have Been Excluded

None of the figures I have presented includes charges for room and board expenses, which averaged $3,670 and $4,716 at public and private

Table 2-2. *Tuition, Grants, and Student Loans for Full-Time Undergraduates, by Type of Institution, 1992–93*

Current dollars

| Parental income | Tuition and fees | Grant aid | | | Net tuition | Loan aid | |
		Federal	State	College funds		Student loans	Parental loans (PLUS)
Full-time public two-year colleges							
< 10,000	902	848	234	94	–279	200	0
10,000–19,999	1,073	807	249	131	–121	234	0
20,000–29,999	986	620	146	98	73	150	23
30,000–39,999	1,122	136	84	139	693	128	86
40,000–49,999	1,173	19	38	129	952	151	70
50,000–59,999	1,220	10	29	79	1,085	19	0
60,000–69,999	1,268	0	0	33	1,228	110	15
70,000–79,999	1,227	0	0	27	1,148	0	0
80,000–99,999	1,195	0	0	70	1,122	160	0
100,000+	1,200	6	0	0	1,186	0	0
Full-time public four-year colleges							
< 10,000	2,401	1,796	588	239	–287	1,172	147
10,000–19,999	2,278	1,476	522	264	–79	1,380	81
20,000–29,999	2,304	789	417	314	672	1,158	150
30,000–39,999	2,459	277	254	261	1,596	997	183
40,000–49,999	2,449	125	146	316	1,765	778	275
50,000–59,999	2,449	29	97	173	2,070	399	181
60,000–69,999	2,531	13	50	161	2,238	207	138
70,000–79,999	2,513	12	26	247	2,190	271	120
80,000–99,999	2,557	10	37	184	2,250	186	172
100,000+	2,706	5	75	175	2,423	116	125
Full-time private four-year colleges							
< 10,000	8,992	2,235	1,036	2,096	3,423	2,215	233
10,000–19,999	9,367	1,891	1,073	2,974	3,142	2,138	313
20,000–29,999	9,928	1,061	916	3,174	4,532	2,463	407
30,000–39,999	10,975	492	545	3,418	5,972	2,264	382
40,000–49,999	11,162	259	543	4,109	5,818	2,108	476
50,000–59,999	11,487	94	236	3,321	7,558	1,516	373
60,000–69,999	12,108	12	76	1,655	10,170	941	234
70,000–79,999	12,489	26	57	1,559	10,707	939	294
80,000-99,999	12,118	14	77	1,783	10,050	1,179	286
100,000+	13,141	10	28	943	12,078	317	138

Source: Author's calculations based on data from the National Postsecondary Student Aid Study, 1992–93, restricted use data file.

four-year colleges, respectively, in 1992.[26] The reason they have been excluded is that it is difficult to identify any increase in living costs accrued because a person is enrolled in college. He or she would be eating, drinking, and needing a place to sleep even if not in school. It is true that there may be some incremental housing cost imposed on the families of students who maintain an apartment or dormitory room at school as well as a room at their parent's home during the summer. However, these costs may be offset somewhat if the economies of scale enjoyed by dining halls allow students to eat for less than the cost to parents buying groceries and cooking at home. And although many parents have to write checks to pay the salaries of those who are serving in locus parenti, those same parents are also saving themselves some of the tribulations of having their adolescent children living in their home. By excluding room and board charges I may be understating the costs of college somewhat, but the amount depends on how much parents value peace of mind.

"Net Progressivity" of Federal, State, and Institutional Subsidies

Financial aid formulas and data on financial aid recipients can leave the strong impression that public subsidies for higher education are highly targeted on those with low family incomes. But this impression could be mistaken. First, college enrollment rates vary dramatically by family income. Although financial aid formulas grant more aid to low-income students when they get to college, higher-income youth are generally more likely to attend college and are more likely to benefit from the aid. And among those attending college, higher-income students are more likely to attend elite public institutions, which receive larger subsidies per student than the typical community college. Access to an elite public university education in Ann Arbor, Michigan, or Berkeley, California, or Chapel Hill, North Carolina, is not directly means tested, but admission is contingent on such factors as high school grades and standardized test scores, which are often correlated with family income. Finally, higher-income youth remain in college longer than than those from lower-income families. In this section I try to sort out the net effect

26. National Center for Education Statistics (1997b, table 312).

of each of these factors on the distribution of public postsecondary education subsidies by family income.

Public support for higher education comes in a number of different ways, and no single accounting system keeps track of the sources. Table 2-3 shows the targeting of public education subsidies from financial aid as well as state and local operating subsidies to institutions among those students attending college in a given year. Data on revenues from state and local government appropriations per full-time-equivalent student were merged with the 1992–93 National Postsecondary Student Aid Study data.[27] Because I am primarily interested in the distribution of financial aid subsidies, I have focused on dependent students, for whom parental income information is available. The subsidies on state and federal loans were estimated to be one-third of the loan value. State and federal grant aid includes institutional grant aid for those attending public institutions.

Reflecting the means testing in the calculation of eligibility for aid programs, public subsidies provided through grant and loan programs decrease steeply as family income increases. Students from families with annual incomes less than $13,000 received $1,848 in state and federal grant aid, ten times more than those from families with incomes greater than $90,000. Lower-income families also received considerably more state and federal loans.

However, the magnitude of state and local subsidies received by college students is less dependent on family income. In fact, the average postsecondary student from a family with an income greater than $90,000 received $2,114 in subsidies from state and local appropriations, only $324 larger than the $1,790 appropriation subsidy received by the lowest-income youths. This fact may be surprising because low-income students are more likely to attend two-year colleges, which often receive smaller subsidies than four-year colleges. However, higher-income students are also more likely to attend private institutions, which essentially offsets any difference in subsidies received by high-income students attending high-subsidy public institutions.

27. Part-time students were assumed to receive one-third of the state and local appropriation per student received by full-time students. The appropriations do not distinguish between those provided to graduate and undergraduate education. As a result, I implicitly assumed that the subsidy is shared by graduate and undergraduate students in proportion to their enrollments. The actual value of the loan subsidies will depend on prevailing interest rates and the length of time a student remains in school.

Table 2-3. *Public Subsidies to College Students, by Type of Subsidy and Family Income, 1992–93*[a]

Current dollars unless otherwise indicated

Parental income	State and federal grant aid (1)	State and federal loan aid (2)	State and local appropriations (3)	Total annual subsidy per student (4)	Percent entering college (5)	Years of enrollment (6)	Total subsidy (4×5×6)
0–12,999	1,848	334	1,790	3,972	39.0	3.11	4,812
13,000–24,999	1,132	266	1,813	3,211	53.5	3.35	5,750
25,000–34,999	719	252	1,929	2,900	55.8	3.45	5,573
35,000–44,999	352	164	1,549	2,066	64.3	3.44	4,559
45,000–64,999	243	129	2,145	2,517	72.0	3.83	6,927
65,000–89,999	172	136	1,965	2,273	82.2	4.12	7,647
90,000+	161	50	2,114	2,325	89.8	4.41	9,195

Sources: Author's calculations. The estimates combine data from the National Postsecondary Student Aid Survey in 1992–93 with data from the Integrated Postsecondary Education Data System on state and local appropriations per student.

a. Students at any public or private two-year or four-year college or proprietary school were included. Part-time students were allocated one-third of the state and local appropriation per student. Independent students were excluded. Data on college entry rates were drawn from the 1994 follow-up of the National Education Longitudinal Study sample of eighth-grade students in 1988; the students were two years out of high school. Data on academic years of enrollment were drawn from the High School and Beyond survey of high school sophomores in 1980 when they were followed up in 1992. Years of enrollment does not refer to years of college completed, but the number of years during which a student reported some enrollment. Total subsidy numbers do not compute exactly because of rounding.

Column 4 in table 2-3 provides an estimate of the aggregated public subsidy per college student. Among those in college, the progressivity built into the grant and loan programs is large enough to outweigh the lack of progressivity in state and local subsidies. Low-income students are estimated to receive an average of $3,972 a year in total public subsidies as compared with $2,325 a year for those from families with incomes above $90,000.

But once again, students with different family incomes have very different probabilities of entering college. They also remain in college for different lengths of time. Given their greater likelihood of being prepared to enter and remain in college, higher-income youth can actually expect to receive larger public subsidies for their education than those from lower-income families. Despite the targeting of aid, students from families with incomes greater than $90,000 can expect to receive nearly twice the subsidy provided to those from families with incomes less than $13,000. As table 2-3 shows, the reason is that the higher-income students are more than twice as likely to enter college in the first place: 90 percent of those from families with incomes higher than $90,000 enrolled in college within two years after graduating from high school as opposed to 39 percent of those from families with incomes less than $13,000. And they can expect to be enrolled in college for longer: among those ever entering college, young people from high-income families were enrolled at some point more than 4.41 years as compared with 3.11 years for the lowest-income entrants.

State Subsidies to Two-Year and Four-Year Colleges

Although only ten state legislatures explicitly set tuition at public institutions (either by practice or statute), differences in state appropriations per student go a long way toward explaining differences in tuitions at public institutions.[28] In the typical state, a higher education coordinating or governing board sets tuition rates for resident students based on a comparison of state appropriations and costs. In 1995, state and local appropriations accounted for 65 percent of educational costs at the average public four-year institution and 84 percent at public two-year

28. Based on a survey of state higher education executive officers reported in Christal (1997). The states were California, Colorado, Florida, Indiana, New York, North Carolina, Oklahoma, South Dakota, Texas, and Washington.

institutions.[29] Indeed, until the mid-1980s, many states arrived at their higher-education budgets based on formulas involving enrollments as well as actual costs. When the formulas were in use, appropriations grew automatically as costs and enrollments grew. However, the budget crises of the late 1980s forced many states to reconsider their investments in higher education. As postsecondary enrollments grew, state appropriations typically did not keep pace, leading to increases in public college tuition.

To the extent that greater public subsidies to higher education mean higher state sales and income taxes (as opposed to other cuts in state spending), one might think of such subsidies as a crude income-contingent loan program. A college education requires an intensive use of society's resources during a relatively brief period. Because families may have difficulty amassing such savings before their children enter college, societies traditionally have helped them smooth their consumption by subsidizing higher education and asking families to pay higher taxes.

This is only a crude system, since families move across state borders and, until recently, only about half of high school graduates went to college. However, one advantage of such a form of financing is that the marginal tax rate required to pay for the subsidy is lower than the tax rates implicit in the financial aid formulas, because the tax is paid over a lifetime of state income tax rather than a single year of parental income or assets. For instance, table 2-1 shows that someone from a four-person family with income of $20,000 and assets of $25,000 would have an expected family contribution of zero. Such a person would qualify for the maximum Pell Grant of $3,000. But someone from a family with similar assets but with income of $40,000 would have an expected family contribution of just over $3,000 and would not qualify for a Pell Grant. In other words, in the $20,000 to $40,000 range of income, families would lose a benefit of $3,000, implying a marginal tax rate of 15 percent over that income range from the student financial aid formula alone.

What tax rate would be required to provide a similar benefit to college students through an across-the-board subsidy? Obviously, it would require very little change in marginal tax rates to raise the $6 billion

---

29. Educational costs are the same as those defined earlier. Costs are based on author's calculations using data from the the Integrated Postsecondary Education Data System.

budget of the Pell Grant program. But that is not a fair comparison since, presumably, the benefits could not be similarly targeted without explicitly means-testing the benefit. (If the benefits could be targeted to the same students without "taxing" income explicitly, this would obviously be preferred to either means-tested aid or across-the-board subsidies.) Rather, the fair comparison would be to ask what increase in a broad-based tax would be required to provide a $3,000 across-the-board benefit to all students attending public institutions. In 1995 there were 7.8 million full-time-equivalent students attending public institutions, meaning that a $3,000 across-the-board subsidy would cost $23.3 billion. Such a sum could have been raised with an additional 0.4 percentage point increase in average state tax rates in 1995.[30] Because the distortionary effect of taxes increases with the square of the tax rate, raising general taxes by 0.4 percentage point may, in the end, have less of a distortionary effect on behavior than imposing a 15 percent implicit marginal tax rate through the means-tested Pell Grant program.[31] Therefore, the more one worries about the tax rates in the student aid system, the more one might be tempted to favor across-the-board subsidies.

Description of New Tax Benefits

In August 1997 Congress and the president created new tax expenditures to offset the costs of college and encourage families to save more for higher education.[32] Families with students in their first two years of college could receive a tax credit of up to $1,500 a student for tuition expenses. This credit, referred to as the Hope Scholarship credit, is provided on 100 percent of tuition expenses (less any federal, state, or private grant aid) up to $1,000 and 50 percent of any remaining tuition expenses up to $2,000. Room and board expenses do not count for the credit. Eligibility is phased out for families with incomes between $80,000 and $100,000 and for single filers with incomes between $40,000 and $50,000.

30. Personal income in 1995 was $6.1 trillion. Council of Economic Advisers (1997, table B-25). The number of full-time-equivalent students is from National Center for Education Statistics (1997b, table 200).

31. The rule of thumb that the distortionary impact of a tax increases with the square of the tax rate is described in Rosen (1992, p. 316).

32. Much of the discussion of tax expenditure policy in this section is drawn from Kane (1998).

Students taking classes beyond their first two years of college are eligible to receive a 20 percent credit on the first $5,000 of out-of-pocket tuition expenses. The maximum, which will be raised to $10,000 in 2003, applies to each taxpaying unit, not to each student. The income eligibility limits will be the same as for the Hope Scholarship credit, and neither tax credit can be refunded if the credit exceeds a family's tax liability.

Parents will also be able to withdraw funds from existing IRA accounts to pay tuition or room and board. Withdrawals for these expenses will not be subject to a 10 percent penalty as they would have been before passage of the act. However, as would be true at withdrawal on retirement for the classic IRA, the distributions are considered taxable income.

In addition, children under age 18 can have $500 a year deposited in their behalf to help pay future tuition and room and board expenses. Single taxpayers with incomes less than $110,000 or joint-filing taxpayers with incomes less than $160,000 can make such contributions. The contributions to an education IRA are not deductible, but distributions (both principal and capital gains) are excluded from income as long as they are used to pay college expenses. Any balances not used for college are distributed as taxable income to the child at age 30. The beneficiary must pay a 10 percent penalty on such unused balances.[33]

Parents or students can deduct up to $1,000 in interest on loans used to pay education expenses. This limit will be raised in $500 increments to $2,500 in 2001. Eligibility for the deduction will be phased out for joint filers with incomes between $60,000 and $75,000 and for single filers between $40,000 and $55,000.

Student loans provided by tax-exempt organizations such as universities or state governments can now be forgiven with no tax liability for the beneficiary as long as the person is working for a tax-exempt organization or governmental unit in an "underserved" occupation or geographic area. In the past, graduates would have had to pay federal income tax on loans that were forgiven, with the exception of some special federal loan programs.

Finally, participants in state-run prepaid tuition plans will receive a relatively small incremental benefit. Previously, funds could be withdrawn to pay the cost of tuition. Now such funds can also be used to

---

33. Balances can also be transferred to any younger siblings.

pay room and board. Participants will still pay a tax on any capital gains at withdrawal. The primary tax advantage offered by such plans—that no tax is paid on their income until withdrawal—will remain in place.

The Effects of the New Tax Expenditures

The final tax expenditure legislation improved on earlier proposals. Congress wisely dropped the requirement that students must maintain a B average to qualify for the tax credit. In addition to the administrative difficulties in asking the Internal Revenue Service to confirm student transcripts, the hoped-for benefits were not obvious. Indeed, given the likelihood of grade inflation and grade-conscious course choices by risk-averse students, the response may even have been detrimental. Still, a number of difficulties remain.

First, the tax benefits are simply not well targeted. The new tax expenditures offer low-income families very little. Because neither of the tax credits is refundable, a family must have a substantial federal tax liability to qualify for them. And because only out-of-pocket expenses are counted—tuition minus any grants received—the proposal simply reduces the progressivity of existing means-tested formulas. The estimated cost of these new tax expenditures is $41 billion over the first five years, making them roughly the same size as the primary federal means-tested grant program, and virtually all of the expenditures will go to middle- and higher-income families.

Second, because the $1,500 tax credit provides a 100 percent credit on the first $1,000 in out-of-pocket expenses and effectively does not require any copayment on expenses up to $1,000, it will encourage eligible institutions to offer leisure-oriented courses for college credit to taxpayers qualifying for the subsidy. As long as such courses cost less than $1,000 and could superficially qualify for degree credits, those attending them will be fully reimbursed. For instance, colleges could offer $1,000 whale-watching tours to taxpayers as long as they granted them half-time credit toward a marine biology degree. Because the IRS cannot be expected to monitor course content, the tax credit is likely to fund a large number of frivolous adult education courses.

Third, those institutions with tuition less than $5,000 will have an incentive to relabel room and board charges as tuition charges to qualify them for the tax credit, thereby raising the estimated cost of the proposal. Under previous law, there was no incentive for colleges to shift room and board expenses into tuition charges because they were treated the same in the student aid formulas. However, those colleges with current tuition charges of less than $5,000 (primarily public institutions) will be tempted to charge on-campus students "tuition" for access to dormitory study halls and so forth. About a fifth of the 6 million students at public four-year colleges live on campus and pay room and board charges averaging over $4,000.[34] Relabeling would be less of a concern at private institutions because their tuition is generally above $5,000 already.

Despite the fears of some of the plan's critics (and, perhaps, even contrary to the secret hopes of some of the plan's supporters in the academic world), the legislation is unlikely to lead to rampant tuition inflation, at least at high-cost institutions. The reason: although it may provide welcome tax relief to families, it has little effect on the marginal cost to families when an institution raises tuition. The few institutions with tuitions less than $1,000 will have a clear incentive to raise tuition, since students in families with sufficient taxable income would be paying nothing on the margin. Likewise, those with tuition between $1,000 and $2,000 will be receiving 50 percent tax subsidies to cover the cost. However, those with out-of-pocket tuition costs greater than $2,000 will be receiving at most 20 percent on the margin for tuition increases up to $5,000. (Indeed, first- and second-year students at such institutions will be paying 100 percent of any tuition increase because they would be expected to be taking the Hope Scholarship credit rather than the other type of credit.) Above $5,000, families would be paying 100 percent of any tuition increase. Although many institutions may be tempted to raise tuition, the prospect of declining enrollments or, at public institutions, the political resistance of angry parents may well constrain colleges' options.

Where competition reigns the proposal is unlikely to have much of an effect on colleges' financial aid awards either. Only students with tuition minus grant expenditures of less than $1,500 and greater than zero will be reimbursed by more than 50 percent if the institution cuts its grant award. Those students receiving grant aid larger than the tuition bill (therefore covering part of their living expenses) and those receiving grants more than $1,500 less than the full cost of tuition would not be reimbursed if an institution cut its aid package.

---

34. National Center for Education Statistics (1995; 1997b, tables 173, 312).

The primary impact of the tax expenditures will be an income effect rather than a price effect, as if the federal government were sending families a tax refund unrelated to how much more they spend on college. In fact, it *is* unrelated on the margins where most families are deciding where to send their children to college because most are already paying more than the specified limits. Families will spend some of this tax saving on higher education, but they are likely to spend most of it on other consumption—a summer vacation or new furniture. Colleges may capture a portion of the benefit when families choose to consume more education with their tax windfall, particularly those colleges with considerable market power. But in the end, relatively little of the tax relief is likely to show up in faculty salaries, dormitory repairs, or library acquisitions. The higher education provisions of the Taxpayer Relief Act of 1997 are just that—taxpayer relief, not education policy.

The Tax Expenditures and National Savings

In anticipating the likely effects of the new tax expenditures on savings behavior, I find it helpful to divide the problem into three questions. What is the likely effect of the new tax expenditures on withdrawals from existing IRA accounts? What are the implications of the new education IRA on new parental saving for college? And what is the effect on the relative cost of parental saving and student borrowing?

The Reforms and Existing IRA Accounts

Allowing penalty-free use of IRA savings for college may not in the end have a large effect on IRA balances. The simple reason is that most families are likely to have access to less costly sources of capital than withdrawing from their tax-advantaged retirement accounts. The least expensive source of capital for most families is likely to be subsidized student loans because the federal government pays the interest while a student is enrolled in school. Where college expenses would exceed the sum of expected family contributions and any grant aid that might be received, dependent students can borrow up to $2,625 their first year, $3,500 their second, and $5,500 a year during subsequent years under the federal student loan program. Moreover, for those with access to other forms of capital, there is no penalty for paying off the loan immediately after graduation.

For parents who are homeowners, home equity is likely to be the next pool of capital. In 1997 the average yield on new home mortgages was 7.71 percent.[35] And the deductibility of mortgage interest makes home equity an even more attractive source of capital. Because of the savings provided by mortgage interest deductibility, the effective cost of capital in 1997 would have been 5.5 percent using home equity for those in the 28 percent tax bracket.

For those who are not homeowners, the third source of capital is likely to be the Parent Loans for Undergraduate Students program. Once a family has borrowed the maximum allowable under the subsidized program, it has access to PLUS (or unsubsidized loans to students). Under PLUS, the cost of borrowing has been equal to the bond equivalent rate of the ninety-one-day Treasury bill plus 3.1 percent. In recent years the interest rate on the loans has been between 8 and 8.5 percent.

All these sources of capital are likely to be less expensive than the opportunity cost of withdrawing funds from an IRA, where money accumulates tax free until withdrawal. A parent ten years from retirement, for example, with a marginal tax rate of 28 percent and earning the historical nominal return on equities (12.7 percent a year since 1926 based on Standard & Poor's 500 index), the opportunity cost of withdrawing from an IRA would be to forgo an after-tax rate of return on that investment of 9.1 percent a year.

What does all this imply about net increases in IRA savings (as opposed to withdrawals from existing accounts) in anticipation of college bills? Suppose that a parent has not already contributed the maximum but is considering contributing more to an IRA. The option of being able to withdraw IRA funds to pay college expenses is only valuable to the extent that families do not have other less expensive sources of capital available. Thus when it comes time for their children to enroll in college, many parents are going to find that it is less expensive to borrow using student loans or home equity loans than to withdraw funds from their tax-advantaged IRAs. Therefore, families are unlikely to save more in their IRAs to pay for college.

All of these conclusions presume that the transaction costs of withdrawing from an IRA are at least as high as the shoe leather costs of taking out a home equity or PLUS loan. The larger the hassle costs of veri-

---

35. Council of Economic Advisers (1998, table B-73).

fying eligibility for penalty-free distributions for college expenses, the smaller the effects are likely to be on existing IRA savings.

The Education IRA and the Payoff to Parental Savings

At first glance one might be tempted to conclude that the new education IRAs represent an important tax-advantaged savings vehicle for parents saving for college. However, a more careful reading of the rules makes it clear that the program raises the payoff to saving only for parents with young children that are planning to send them to expensive colleges. The primary reason is that the parent making a withdrawal from an education IRA forgoes eligibility for the Hope Scholarship tax credit as well as the 20 percent Lifetime Learning tax credit for a student for that year. The Hope Scholarship tax credit is worth up to $1,500 a year for the first two years of college; the Lifetime Learning credit is worth up to $1,000 a year for those attending institutions with tuitions greater than $5,000. (In five years, when the maximum countable tuition expense is raised from $5,000 to $10,000, the Lifetime Learning tax credit will be worth $2,000 a year.) As a result, the availability of the education IRA presents a potential net gain only for those who can expect a tax benefit greater than $1,500 a year for the first two years and $1,000 a year for subsequent years. Otherwise, a parent is better off simply claiming the tax credit at the time of attendance and using other financial vehicles such as a mutual fund to save.

Consider the following example. If it is five years before my child can attend college, I have a choice between making use of the education IRA or not making a deposit in an education IRA and waiting to take advantage of the Hope Scholarship tax credit. Suppose that I face a marginal tax rate of 28 percent and a pretax nominal rate of return of 12.7 percent. If I were to save $500 each year for the next five years, I would be able to accrue $354 more in my tax-advantaged education IRA account than I could have by putting the same resources into a mutual fund account, which has no tax advantages. However, to capture this $354 in tax savings, I would have to forgo the $1,500 in tax savings available through the Hope Scholarship tax credit. Obviously, I would be better off abstaining from the education IRA and simply claiming the Hope Scholarship when it comes time for my child to attend college.

Table 2-4 compares the accumulated value of depositing $500 each year in an education IRA beginning one to seventeen years before a

Table 2-4. *Tax Advantage from Making the Maximum Annual Contribution to the Education IRA, by Starting Year*

Current dollars

	Accumulated savings at college entry		
Years before college	Education IRA	Non-tax-advantaged saving	Difference
17	29,432	20,446	8,986
16	25,615	18,233	7,382
15	22,228	16,205	6,023
14	19,224	14,348	4,876
13	16,557	12,646	3,911
12	14,191	11,086	3,105
11	12,092	9,657	2,435
10	10,230	8,348	1,882
9	8,577	7,149	1,428
8	7,110	6,050	1,060
7	5,809	5,043	766
6	4,654	4,121	533
5	3,630	3,275	355
4	2,721	2,501	220
3	1,914	1,791	123
2	1,199	1,141	58
1	564	546	18

Source: Author's calculations, using an annual pretax rate of return of 12.7 percent, $500 savings each year, and a marginal tax rate of 28 percent.

child enters college as opposed to a savings vehicle without tax advantages. The calculations assume a marginal tax rate of 28 percent and an annual pretax return of 12.7 percent. The far right column shows the difference in value of the education IRA when compared with another form of savings at the time of college entry when a parent would be forgoing other tax credits. The education IRA offers tax advantages less than $1,500 unless a parent begins saving $500 a year ten years or more before sending a child to college. However, the parent would also have to expect to be spending slightly more than $10,000 a year on tuition and room and board to be able to take advantage of the credit. If I expect my child to attend a low-tuition public institution, I am likely to be better off not saving in the education IRA and simply claiming the Hope Scholarship tax credit at the time of enrollment. (Although the Hope tax credit is available only for the first two years, those who are eligible for it will be eligible for up to $1,000 a year for the Lifetime Learning credit in subsequent years.) To the extent that parents are uncertain about which type of college their child is likely to attend or whether the child is likely to attend at all, they may also value the option of keeping their savings in a regular savings account. Even with a 12.7 percent pre-tax return on their investment, the education IRA offers no incremental savings incentive for parents whose children are less than ten years away from college or who expect their children to attend institutions costing less than $10,000 a year.[36]

The Tax Expenditures and the Relative Cost of Capital

The new tax expenditures allow parents or students with incomes below $40,000 for single filers and $60,000 for joint filers to deduct up to $1,000 a year in interest paid on educational loans. (The limit will be raised annually in $500 increments to $2,500 a year by 2001.) For those who could benefit from either the education IRA or the deductibility of student loan interest, the results are symmetric. Therefore for those who are qualified for either benefit, it is ambiguous whether the combination of the two would lead to more parental saving or more student or parental borrowing, except, of course, when the marginal tax rate facing parents is higher than the marginal tax rate facing students.

However, for those who qualify for the deductibility of college loan interest payments and not the educational IRA, the combination lowers the cost of borrowing more than it raises the payoff to parental saving. Ironically, although the goal of these policies was to encourage parents to save more to help pay tuition bills, the net result may be to encourage them to save less and students to borrow more to finance college.

---

36. There may be a few exceptions. Both the tuition tax credit and the education IRA are phased out for youth from higher-income families. However, grandparents are allowed to contribute to education IRA accounts and the income phaseouts are faster for the tuition tax credit than for the education IRA. Parents filing jointly with incomes between $100,000 and $160,000 (who are eligible to contribute to the education IRA but not to take the tax credits) or parents with incomes greater than $160,000 whose own parents (children's grandparents) have incomes less than $160,000 may receive tax-advantaged savings returns from the education IRA even if their children are less than ten years away from college or expect to attend inexpensive public institutions. Moreover, those with more than one child in college could benefit more from the education IRA than from the other tax credits.

The Tax Expenditures and College Investment Behavior

The new tax expenditures unambiguously lower the cost of borrowing for students and have ambiguous effects on the payoff to savings for parents concerned about paying for their children's education. What is the likely effect on aggregate investments in college? There are two additional ways in which parents and students may be adjusting their behavior: more young people may decide to enter college and those who already know they are going to enroll may be willing to attend more expensive institutions. The Hope Scholarship tax credit has dramatic implications for the marginal cost of college tuition for those currently paying less than $1,000; that is, for those with tax liabilities against which to count the credit, it lowers the cost of the tuition portion of college expenses to zero (although students still face the cost of forgone earnings). Between $1,000 and $2,000, the Hope Scholarship credit lowers the marginal cost of a dollar in tuition to $.50. For both reasons it provides powerful incentives for states to consider raising community college tuition levels and for students to attend more expensive institutions. To the extent that state and local governments raise tuition levels to capture more of the federal tax credit, the tax expenditures are merely a disguised block grant to the states. Indeed, policymakers in states such as Massachusetts and California are already considering tailoring their tuition policies to take advantage of the new federal tax expenditures.[37]

However, above $2,000 the program has relatively minor effects on the marginal cost of attending college. Between $2,000 and $5,000 the program lowers the marginal cost by 20 percent. Above $5,000 the tax credits affect the marginal cost of attending a more expensive institution only through the deductibility of loan interest.

For those already planning to pay more than $2,000 a year in tuition, the primary result of the tax expenditures is an income effect, not a price effect. To the extent that such families are wealthier as a result of the tax expenditures, they may spend more of that wealth on college. But they are also likely to spend much of the windfall on food, vacations, or even patio furniture.

37. For example, see Patrick Healy, "Massachusetts Considers Mixing Federal and State Aid to Cut Costs at 2-Year Colleges," *Chronicle of Higher Education*, September 26, 1997, p. A34; and Julianne Basinger and Patrick Healy, "Will New Federal Tax Breaks Hurt California's Colleges?" *Chronicle of Higher Education*, March 6, 1998, p. A36.

How Other Countries Pay for College

Industrialized countries have taken different approaches to rationing resources for postsecondary training. The two main instruments for affecting access are tuition policies and admission standards. The strategies tend to be substitutes for one another. Where tuition is very low or nonexistent, societies erect other hurdles to limit access, such as requiring passage of a national exam at the end of high school. When students pay a larger share of the price themselves, those who are least likely to benefit from a postsecondary education have a stronger incentive to select themselves out, and there is less need for a restrictive admission standard.

Among the industrialized nations, only the United States, Japan, and Korea finance more than half of postsecondary expenditures (the direct costs, not forgone earnings) by private means.[38] European countries have traditionally had very low tuition or, more often, none at public institutions.[39] However, given the global trend of widening earnings differentials between the more and less educated, the proportion of youth seeking postsecondary training has increased dramatically in most industrialized countries. Postsecondary enrollment per capita more than doubled between 1975 and 1995 in ten of the seventeen countries for which data were available (table 2-5). The United States and Sweden are the only industrialized countries where the percentage of full-time-equivalent college students per one hundred persons aged 5 to 29 increased by one-third or less for the two decades.

Without tuition, postsecondary institutions depend on public subsidies as their main source of revenue. During times such as these, with rapidly increasing demand, quality of education can suffer because revenues are less directly tied to the number of students demanding attention. As a result, the rise in college enrollments has recently forced some countries to abandon their zero-tuition policies and raise tuition as a means of providing greater resources to higher education institutions. In spring 1998 students in Britain protested the Blair government's proposal to charge $1,700 in tuition at public institutions, a modest sum by U.S. standards.[40]

38. Organization for Economic Cooperation and Development (1997, p. 56).
39. Organization for Economic Cooperation and Development (1997, table B3.3).
40. "Students in Britain Protest New Fees," *Chronicle of Higher Education*, March 13, 1998, p. A55.

Table 2-5. *Full-Time Students Enrolled in Postsecondary Institutions as a Percentage of Persons Aged 5–29, by Country, 1975, 1995*

Country	1975	1995	Percent change
North America			
Canada	6.7	11.2	67
United States	6.6	8.7	32
Pacific area			
Australia	4.5	6.4	42
Japan	4.3	8.7	102
New Zealand	2.5	7.0	180
Europe			
Austria	2.9	8.6	197
Denmark	6.1	10.1	66
Finland	5.0	12.6	152
France	4.9	10.3	110
Germany	4.4	8.3	89
Greece	3.4	8.2	141
Ireland	2.4	6.4	167
Italy	4.6	9.6	109
Netherlands	4.9	7.7	57
Spain	3.7	10.6	186
Sweden	5.6	6.4	14
United Kingdom	2.5	5.8	132

Source: Organization for Economic Cooperation and Development (1997, p. 142).

Although they differ in their reliance on tuition financing, virtually every industrialized country depends on some mixture of direct public subsidies to public institutions and means-tested aid to students from low-income families. But in 1989 Australia implemented a very different form of means-tested aid.[41] Rather than base the amount on a backward-looking assessment of a family's resources, public subsidies were provided on a forward-looking basis, using a student's earnings after college. For instance, in 1996 the undergraduate students were charged a uniform tuition of $1,900 (U.S. dollars), regardless of their family resources.[42] (The amount covers roughly one-quarter of costs, the remainder being provided by public subsidies.) No interest is charged while a student is enrolled, so that after four years the typical student

41. For more details on the Australian system, see Chapman (1997).
42. Using an exchange rate of $.778 U.S. per Australian dollar.

would graduate with a tuition debt of $7,600. After graduation, students repay at rates of 3 to 5 percent of any income they receive in excess of the average taxable income of Australian workers. Graduates stop paying into the Higher Education Contribution Scheme (HECS) once they have paid off their debts. Because the interest rate charged is simply equal to the rate of inflation (a zero real rate), those with the lowest incomes receive the largest subsidies. The imposition of student charges when combined with the HECS does not appear to have a disproportionate impact on low-income students.[43]

Conclusion

As a college education increases in economic importance, the nation's system for financing higher education, that mysterious province of college financial aid officers, federal and state department of education specialists, and private banks and guarantee agencies, has a subtle but decisive influence on the nation's economic future. After all, how we pay for college helps determine who goes and, possibly, what they choose to study. As a result, the labyrinthine financial aid system quietly influences not only how many faculty members are hired but also the pace of economic growth and the distribution of economic rewards.

The U.S. system for financing higher education has relied on two basic forms of aid: large operating subsidies to public institutions and backward-looking means-tested grants and loans. Each form has strengths and weaknesses. The large operating subsidies for postsecondary institutions are easier for hard-pressed families to anticipate than the complicated financial need calculations. And to the extent that they are paid for with broad-based taxes, they do not require the same high marginal tax rates implicit in targeted means-tested aid programs. However, when public subsidies cover a large share of the cost, families and students have less incentive to spend society's educational resources prudently. Although there are likely to be general social benefits to higher education that families would not consider when making enrollment decisions, it would be difficult to argue that, on the margin, the benefits represent two-thirds of the value of a year of college education, the proportion of costs that states pay at public four-year institutions.

43. Chapman (1997).

Moreover, when eligibility for public largesse depends solely on the ability to earn admission to college, across-the-board subsidies are bound to benefit higher-income students disproportionately because they are more likely to have the academic preparation to enroll in college and to stay longer.

An underemphasized weakness of backward-looking means-tested benefits is that until a person actually applies for college it is unclear just how much aid is available. To the extent that the only beneficiaries are those who were planning to go to college anyway, the program is purely a transfer program and does not encourage low-income young people to continue their education. Thus there is a necessary trade-off between targeting and transparency. Targeting means that it is simply harder to know the cost of college until one knows more about financial aid eligibility. Given their focus on student aid packaging, tailoring aid to the specific needs of those who have applied for it, financial aid professionals tend to overweight targeting and underweight transparency.

The approach to higher education finance initiated in Australia in 1989 represents a third way, a method of means testing that moves the uncertainty about the magnitude of the subsidies until after college. I will discuss this idea in more detail in chapter 5.

3

Rising Costs in Higher Education

Not so long ago, Nobel prize awards and spring commencement proceedings were the hot news stories in higher education. Now, they have been displaced by the annual tuition announcement as the most closely watched event on the academic calendar. Between 1980 and 1995 tuition increases were certainly large enough to be newsworthy: the average annual increases at public and private four-year institutions were 8.8 and 8.5 percent (in nominal terms), respectively—more than double the average annual increase (4.2 percent) in consumer prices.[1]

The large increases announced during the late 1980s and early 1990s have generated widespread anxiety among parents about their ability to pay for college in the future. If costs were to continue to rise 4.6 percent a year faster than inflation, a parent of an infant born today could expect real tuition costs to more than double by the time the child enters college. A family with an income of $45,000 would have to save 10 percent of its income for eighteen years just to be able to pay for one child to attend four years at the average private institution. Financial planners use such projections to frighten parents with recommended college savings plans that seem out of reach, and indeed would be out of reach for many families. Although it may help the planners to sell their services, it does little to promote a healthy debate over student financial aid policy. In this chapter, I discuss some of the forces underlying the tuition increases.

1. National Center for Education Statistics (1997b, table 312, p. 326).

Costs per Student

Given the intense labor requirements, any type of education, elementary or postsecondary, is very costly to provide. Yet because nine out of ten children in the United States attend publicly funded elementary and secondary schools, most parents have never written a check to pay for education until their children are ready to attend college.

Many parents would be surprised to learn that the average expenditure per student in public elementary and secondary schools in 1994–95 was $6,915.[2] For those not used to paying tuition, this is likely to appear as an impossibly large number—that is, until they start to add up the expenses. In the 1994–95 school year there were 17.3 students in attendance for each full-time-equivalent teacher.[3] With an average teacher salary of $36,609 and employee benefit costs of 27 percent of salary, instructional costs alone would be $2,697 a year for each student. Add in $556 per student for operation and maintenance of the building, $224 for transportation, $233 for food services, $265 for health services, $451 for administration, and $219 for instructional support such as libraries, computer labs, and curriculum development, and one begins to see why the cost of elementary and secondary education is so high.[4]

Having enjoyed "free" tuition for their children for twelve years, many parents are shocked when they see a college tuition bill for the first time. Figure 3-1 shows estimates of educational expenditures per student in postsecondary institutions since 1967. The schools designated as elite four-year institutions include most of the state flagship universities as well as such private colleges as Boston University, Colgate University, Johns Hopkins University, Macalester College, and the University of Notre Dame, and also the Ivy League institutions.[5] "Other" four-year institutions would include Belmont Abbey College,

2. Total expenditure per pupil in average daily attendance. National Center for Education Statistics (1997b, table 169, p. 172).

3. National Center for Education Statistics (1997b, table 64, p. 74).

4. National Center for Education Statistics (1997b, table 77, p. 84; table 39, p. 50; table 163, p. 162).

5. "Elite four-year" colleges includes the Carnegie Foundation categories "research university I and II," "liberal arts colleges I," and "doctoral granting I." "Other four-year" colleges includes "comprehensive colleges and universities I and II," "doctoral granting II," and "liberal arts colleges II." The two-year colleges are also identified using the Carnegie classification (given their small enrollments, private two-year colleges are excluded). Institutions not granting two-year degrees are excluded.

Figure 3-1. *Educational Expenditures per Student, Elementary, Secondary, and Postsecondary, 1967–94*

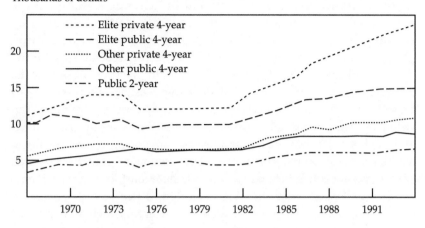

Postsecondary[a]

Thousands of dollars

Public elementary and secondary

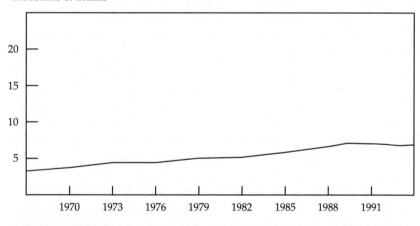

Thousands of dollars

Source: Author's calculations based on postsecondary data from the Integrated Postsecondary Education Data System and per-pupil expenditures in public elementary and secondary schools from National Center for Education Statistics (1997b).

a. Costs were calculated by starting with "educational and general expenditures" reported to the Integrated Postsecondary Education Data System, subtracting expenditures on scholarships and fellowships, and also subtracting revenue from federal, state, and local grants and contracts. Research funded by private foundations could not be distinguished from gifts from private sources and therefore was not excluded. Values were converted to 1995 dollars using the CPI-U.

the California State University system, many of the City University of New York four-year colleges, and Youngstown State University.

These data are drawn from an annual census of postsecondary institutions conducted by the Department of Education. Although the schools may vary somewhat in their accounting practices, the costs are intended to exclude revenues from auxiliary operations such as dormitories, food halls, and hospitals and include costs associated with the educational mission of the institution: faculty salaries, library costs, operations and maintenance of school campuses, and admissions and central administration. Scholarships and fellowships (except those provided by the federal government, such as Pell Grants) have been excluded because they are often transfers from one group of students to another rather than real consumption of economic resources. Research grants and contracts funded by federal, state, and local governments are also excluded since they are intended to fund faculty research instead of teaching. Faculty time spent on research, which is not funded by an outside source, is included in educational costs. (Indeed, one might think of time for unfunded research as a nonmonetary benefit paid to faculty.) Because data are not reported separately for graduate and undergraduate education, both costs and enrollments include graduates and undergraduates. A part-time student was treated as one-third of a full-time student.

The costs per student at different types of institutions have diverged over time. The elite private institutions provide the most expensive education, approximately $22,500 for each full-time-equivalent student in 1994 (1995 dollars). These costs have risen by 85 percent since 1980. Costs at elite public institutions have also increased since 1980 to $14,500 in 1994, but the percentage increase was only half as large as at the private elite institutions.

Outside the elite institutions, costs are less and increases have been much slower. A year at a nonelite private institution was approximately $10,300 in 1994, after rising by 60 percent in real value since 1980. The education cost per year at a nonelite public institution was $8,000 in 1994, rising by 24 percent since 1980. The costs per full-time student at a public two-year college were the lowest ($5,600) but had still risen by 30 percent since 1980. Expenditures per pupil in public elementary and secondary schools ($6,915) were somewhat higher than the cost of a year of community college. However, the percentage increases since 1980 have been similar to the increase at community colleges. Whoever

is actually paying the bill, a year of education is an expensive investment and has become more expensive over the past fifteen years.

Some Facts about Rising College Costs

Any discussion of rising college costs must begin with three fundamental facts: increases in tuition have far outpaced increases in costs;
costs per student have risen across the board, but especially so at private institutions; and private institutions are increasingly providing
grant aid to a larger share of their students, making the "sticker" price—
the price announced in college handbooks as the price before financial
aid—an increasingly misleading indicator of actual costs (table 3-1).

Tuitions at public institutions have increased much more rapidly than
increases in costs. Much of the increase is not the result of an increase in
costs at all but a change in state fiscal policy. In 1980, state and local
appropriations (gross tuition minus institutional scholarship and fellowship aid) covered 83 percent and 76 percent, respectively, of the educational cost per student at public two-year and four-year institutions.
By 1995 the appropriations covered 74 percent and 62 percent. This
decrease has meant large percentage increases in tuition because tuition
covered such a small share of costs in 1980. Even though there was only
a 12 percentage point shift in the proportion of costs covered, the *share* of
costs at public institutions covered by net tuition revenues (less scholarships and fellowships) rose by nearly 60 percent. When considered with
the fact that educational costs per student rose by 28 to 30 percent in real
terms, net tuition nearly doubled at public institutions.

In contrast to what has been happening on public campuses, where
the rise in tuition has largely reflected a shift in state fiscal policy, the rise
in tuition at private institutions has largely been due to a rise in costs per
student. The increase in costs per student at private institutions (73 percent) has been more than twice as large as at public colleges.

A final fact to keep in mind is that private institutions now provide
grant aid to a larger share of their students, meaning that the price and
average net price actually paid by students have diverged. Although the
average sticker price rose by 92 percent in real terms between 1980–81
and 1994–95, net tuition per student (less institutional discounts but not
excluding other sources of financial aid such as Pell Grants) rose by
70 percent. Private institutions have simultaneously been increasing the
price and spending more money on scholarship and fellowship aid. At

Table 3-1. *Costs, Tuition, and State and Local Appropriations per Student, by Type of Institution, 1980–81, 1994–95*[a]

Constant 1996 dollars unless otherwise specified

Tuition and costs	Public two-year			Public four-year			Private four-year		
	1980–81	1994–95	Percent change	1980–81	1994–95	Percent change	1980–81	1994–95	Percent change
Gross tuition per full-time-equivalent student	808	1,693	110	1,840	3,865	110	6,803	13,099	92
Net tuition (less scholarships and fellowships)	690	1,431	107	1,462	3,014	106	5,569	9,484	70
Educational costs per full-time-equivalent student	4,404	5,732	30	8,251	10,604	28	7,679	13,279	73
Shares of educational expenditures (percent per student)									
Net tuition	15.7	25.0	59	18.3	28.8	57	73.5	73.8	0
State and local appropriations	83.3	74.1	–11	76.1	62.0	–18	3.0	1.1	–63
Other	1.0	0.9	–10	5.6	9.2	64	23.5	25.1	7

Source: Author's calculations based on data from the Integrated Postsecondary Education Data System.

a. Educational costs are defined as educational and general expenditures less scholarship and fellowship expenditures and federal, state, local, and private grants and contracts. Part-time students are counted as one-third the value of full-time students when calculating full-time-equivalent enrollments. Figures include both graduate and undergraduate education.

public institutions, which provide much less institutional aid, the increase in net price has more closely mirrored the increase in prices.

Financial Aid Programs and Cost Inflation

The wide availability of federal financial aid has been one of the prime suspects in the hunt for the cause of the price increase in higher education. Tuition, costs, and federal financial aid spending (particularly federal loans) all rose during the 1980s. It is primarily this coincidence in the timing of tuition and loan volume that has led some observers such as Arthur Hauptman and Cathy Krop to suspect that federal policy may have helped cause the increase in expenditures.[6] The circumstantial evidence appears strong: the suspect was certainly in the room at the time of the crime.

Still, such evidence can be misleading. If some other factor were driving up the cost of providing higher education, parents and students would have been forced to borrow more to finance it. In other words, expanding loan volume may not have been the cause of rising educational costs but a reflection of them. More direct evidence is required.

Incentives Implicit in Financial Aid Rules

To diagnose the inflationary influence of federal financial aid programs, one has to study the incentives they provide to colleges to raise tuition and for parents and students to pay more for college. For instance, Pell Grant eligibility is calculated as the maximum Pell Grant (scheduled to be $3,000 for the 1998–99 school year) minus a student's expected family contribution. The tuition charged by a particular school is usually irrelevant in calculating the size of grant that a student receives from the Pell program. The only time tuition matters is when a student's Pell Grant would otherwise exceed the cost of attendance. Since a student's Pell Grant cannot exceed the cost of attendance, his or her award is reduced. For these students who have had their grants reduced, any subsequent increase in tuition is paid for fully by an increase in the grant. But because a student is provided a minimum allowance of $500 for books and a living allowance of $2,500 when living

---

6. Hauptman and Krop (1997).

off campus, a student living off campus would qualify for close to the maximum grant even if tuition was close to zero.[7]

Because tuition generally does not matter for Pell Grant eligibility, students or their parents save 100 percent of any cost difference when they can find a school that costs less, and they pay 100 percent of the increase when their institution raises tuition. Therefore, while a Pell Grant lowers the cost of attending a college, it has no effect on the incremental cost (or savings) of attending a more (or less) expensive institution. For those already planning to attend college, therefore, the program essentially raises a family's income but has little impact on the marginal cost of attending a more expensive school. For those who are considering attending college but are not sure, the program increases demand and, as a result, may have some effect on the prices all colleges can charge. However, in so doing, the Pell Grant program has preserved families' incentives to find the best bargain in higher education that they can.

In contrast to the Pell Grant program, the federal loan program does lower the marginal cost faced by students and parents in choosing a more expensive school, at least up to the amount allowed by the program's loan limits. There are three sources of subsidy: the so-called in-school interest subsidy, which pays the interest on students' loans while they are enrolled in school; the preferential interest rates applied when students begin to pay back the loans; and the lowered cost of default compared with other sources of financing requiring forfeiture of collateral (such as one's house).

Given an alternative source of financing, one can calculate the value of the first two types of price subsidy. Suppose that a family's alternative source of credit is to refinance a home and suppose that their child plans to remain in school for four years. Home mortgage rates peaked at 15.1 percent in 1982.[8] A family borrowing $1,000 in that year to help pay for a student's freshman year in college would have expected to have incurred $511 in after-tax interest charges to carry $1,000 in principal over four years. With the deductibility of mortgage interest, the

7. These minimum costs were eliminated in 1998. However, very few schools are expected to establish living costs that are lower than the former minimums.

8. The interest rate on new home mortgages was drawn from Council of Economic Advisers (1997, table B-71).

effective interest rate would actually have been 10.8 percent [0.151 × (1 – 0.28)] for those in the 28 percent tax bracket. But instead of having $1,511 in freshman tuition and accumulated interest to pay back at the end of four years, the young graduate would have only $1,000 to pay back, because of the federal in-school interest subsidy. Averaging the discount for each of four years of college (and assuming the deductibility of mortgage interest at a 28 percent marginal tax rate), this in-school interest subsidy would reduce by 23 percent the amount a family would owe at the end of four years using the next best source of credit. Then, of course, upon graduation, the student borrower in 1982 would have received an additional subsidy, being allowed to pay off the loan at a preferred 9 percent rate rather than the 15 percent home mortgage rate available at that time.[9] At 1982 interest rates, the combination of the in-school subsidy and the preferential interest rate after graduation would have meant that a family was paying only 46 cents on the dollar for any increase in tuition at schools with tuition charges below the loan limits.[10]

However, there are various reasons to believe that the federal loan programs were not the primary force driving the inflation in both educational costs and tuition. First, the inflation was most pronounced in the late 1980s, after much of the subsidy implicit in the student loan programs had been eliminated. The student loan program was the greatest bargain in 1982, when mortgage interest rates were 15.1 percent and the rate on student loans was 9 percent. By 1986 mortgage interest rates were down to 10.2 percent, implying a 7.34 percent after-tax rate for a family in the 28 percent tax bracket, and the student loan interest rate was 8 percent. Although eligible families continued to receive the subsidy implicit in the in-school interest plan, the gap between private market rates and bargain-basement student loan rates had been reduced dramatically by the mid-1980s.

Probably more important for the relationship of loans and tuition, the marginal price subsidies provided by the student loan programs

9. In the early 1980s both the mortgage interest and the student loan interest charges were deductible. Student loan interest deductibility was eliminated in 1998.

10. This estimate is based on multiplying one minus the average in-school interest subsidy over four years (23 percent) by the ratio of the effective interest rate charged: (1 – 0.23) × (0.09/0.151).

Figure 3-2. *Four-Year Limit on Student Borrowing from Federal Programs, 1976–95*[a]

Constant 1995 dollars

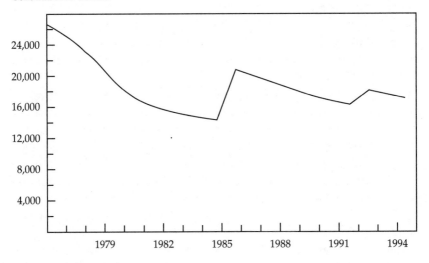

Source: U.S. Department of Education (various years).

a. Figure represents the sum of the loan maximums for a student attending college full time for four consecutive years.

would apply only to expenditures that did not exceed the loan limits.[11] For instance, if a student cannot borrow more than $2,500, the availability of the in-school interest subsidy has no effect on the incremental cost of a tuition increase from $10,000 to $11,000. Moreover, these limits on student borrowing have generally been falling in real value. Between 1976 and 1985 the nominal limit on student borrowing remained $2,500 a year, despite inflation in tuition and other consumer prices. After declining so dramatically in real value, the annual limits on student borrowing were raised in 1986 and in 1992, but they remain lower than they were in the late 1970s (figure 3-2). Yet college tuition and expenditures per student began rising only in the mid-1980s, after the student loan programs had become less of a boon to students and their parents.

11. In fact, the limit on borrowing is equal to the lesser of these limits and the cost of attendance minus the sum of expected family contribution and other financial aid received. For those with unmet financial need less than the borrowing limits, tuition

Finally, because much of the increase in net tuition and expenditure per pupil has been at private four-year institutions, which typically have had tuition charges far above the student loan borrowing limits, loans were unlikely to be driving those increases. In 1982, when student loans were such a bargain, the most a qualified student could borrow to finance a year of college was $2,500 (in 1982 dollars). But the average tuition at a private four-year college was $4,639.[12] When a private college raised its tuition, little of that price difference would have been absorbed by additional borrowing under the federal programs. Similarly, in 1995–96, the most a freshman could borrow under the student loan programs was $2,625, much less than the average private four-year college tuition of $12,243.[13] In other words, when the average private college raised its tuition, most students and families were financing any difference at private rates, not at the lucrative rates available through the subsidized federal student loan program.

The Misleading Analogy to Health Care Cost Inflation

Increased tuitions in higher education have occasionally been compared to rising health care costs. But the economics of federal financial aid policy are very different from the economics of medicaid or medicare. The fundamental problem in fee-for-service health insurance is that neither the patient nor the health care provider faces the marginal cost of additional medical procedures. Fees for visits to a doctor and other forms of copayment are intended to provide incentives for patients to spend health care resources wisely. Indeed, health maintenance organizations were invented to create such cost-containment incentives for health care providers.

Yet because there are limits on Pell Grants and on the amount students can borrow under the subsidized loan programs, virtually every

increases can lead to increases in borrowing eligibility. But my calculations based on the 1992–93 National Postsecondary Student Aid Study suggest that only 13 percent of undergraduate students are limited in borrowing due to "unmet need" and the vast majority of those are constrained by the loan limits themselves. Thus while some student borrowers are eligible for more loan aid as their institution raises tuition, this group contains only a few students.

12. National Center for Education Statistics (1997b, table 312, p. 326).

13. Upperclass students could borrow between $3,500 and $5,500 a year.

student attending a private college and many students attending public institutions are making decisions based on the charges beyond the federal grant and loan limits. These are paid for largely with private resources. Thus federal financial aid policies preserve the incentives for students and their parents to spend educational resources as wisely as possible. Moreover, much of the expense for higher education is not to pay for bricks and mortar and faculty salaries, but represents the forgone earnings of the students, which families are typically paying for themselves.

In an effort to control health care costs, in 1983 Congress dramatically changed the method by which medical providers were reimbursed under the medicare program. Rather than simply paying what the hospitals wanted to charge, the government established a price that they would pay for a given type of service. The introduction of payment by diagnosis represented a dramatic structural change in health care provision, the first of many that continue to transform the industry.

The problem of cost containment in higher education is very different than that in health care provision. The introduction of the prospective payment system in the medicare program was a desperate attempt to reduce the rate of increase in government budgets for health care. If a similar approach were taken in higher education, and the price charged by public and private institutions were frozen at today's levels, for instance, the federal government would save very little. Private institutions already charge tuition far in excess of the limits under the subsidized federal programs. Changes in tuition at these institutions, therefore, have little budgetary impact.

Public institutions may be different. Beacuse their tuition levels are often below the federal grant and loan levels, a rise in tuition at a low-cost public institution very well may mean increases in federal expenditures, particularly in the subsidized student loan programs. But because these tuition increases often come as a result of cuts in state subsidies, it is more appropriate to understand them as a transfer from the federal government to state governments rather than as an increase in the price of higher education, a matter I will discuss in more detail later.

Expanding Loan Volumes since 1992

In the discussion of federal loan subsidies I focused on the subsidized student loan programs. However, beginning in 1981, parents were allowed to supplement student borrowing with borrowing of their own. In 1992 Congress raised the limits on parental borrowing, essentially allowing them to borrow up to the full cost of attendance through the parental loan program (the PLUS program). Higher-income students, who had been excluded from the student loan programs in 1981, were provided access to federally guaranteed loans, known as unsubsidized loans because high-income students would not qualify for the in-school interest subsidy.

Federal college loan volume has risen dramatically since 1992. But most of this increase has been due to expansion of the volume of unsubsidized student and parental loans (figure 3-3).[14] Loan volume under the programs that qualify for the in-school interest subsidy rose from $15.0 billion to $17.9 billion between 1991–92 and 1996–97.[15] However, borrowing under the unsubsidized loan programs increased from $1.4 billion in 1991–92 to $13.2 billion in 1996–97. Therefore, more than three-fourths of the increase was in the unsubsidized programs.

This large increase in borrowing is somewhat puzzling, given that the PLUS loans and unsubsidized Stafford Loans are often more expensive for families than other sources of financing. The average home mortgage rate in 1995 was 7.9 percent. Because mortgage interest can be deducted from income for federal tax purposes, the true cost of using home equity to finance one's college education was lower. For a family in the 28 percent tax bracket, the after-tax cost would be just 5.7 percent. This was actually lower than the rate that was available on federal educational loans for parents (8.38 percent) and on the loans for higher-income students (7.43 percent). Therefore, it is hard to explain the expansion in unsubsidized loan financing since 1992 based on favorable interest rates alone. Perhaps parents and students find it easier, even considering the paperwork to apply for federal student aid, to use the unsubsidized loans than to refinance their homes.[16] Perhaps parents value the option of maintaining home equity to finance potential borrowing needs. How much of the increase in parental borrowing was a net increase in family debt or

14. College Board (1997, table 2).

15. College Board (1998, table 2). In 1991–92 the subsidized Stafford Loan program and Supplemental Loans to Students (SLS) program represented $15 billion in 1997–98 dollars and the PLUS program represented $1.4 billion. In 1996–97 subsidized Stafford Loans (combining direct loans and family education loans) represented $17.9 billion and the unsubsidized and PLUS loans represented $13.2 billion.

16. Of course, parents are likely to attach some value to not being forced to provide their homes as collateral.

Figure 3-3. *Federal Postsecondary Education Loan Program Spending,*
1980–96[a]

Billions of constant 1996 dollars

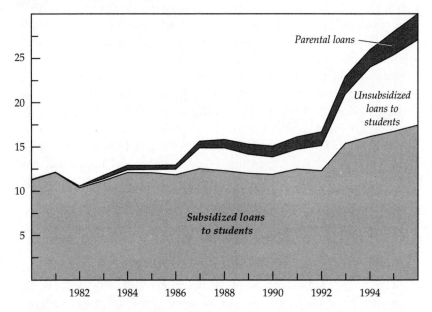

Sources: College Board (1990, 1998).
    a. Subsidized loans include subsidized Stafford Loans. Unsubsidized loans to students include unsubsidized Stafford Loans as well as the Supplemental Loans to Students program. Parental loans include PLUS loans.

simply a shift from other sources of financing remains unclear. But, because of the lack of any significant federal interest rate subsidy, this hardly seems like the place to look for a cause of the tuition increases.

Federal Aid Policy as a Cost-Sharing Plan for State Governments

Although the rise in educational costs was accompanied by increases in federal student loan programs, the federal aid policy is unlikely to have caused the increases. Instead, both may have been driven by other factors. The availability of federal financial aid subsidies may, however, have had a more profound effect on *states'* decisions to limit their own subsidies. The subsidized student loan programs do provide large subsidies at low tuition levels, that is, in the range where public institutions were charging

Figure 3-4. *State Tuition Increases at Public Four-Year Institutions and Medicaid Spending, 1980–94*

Tuition increase (1996 dollars)

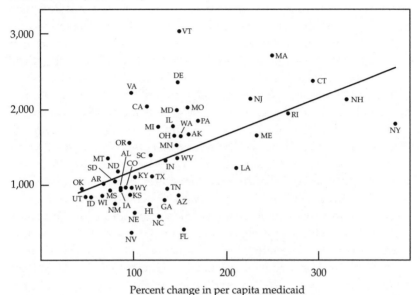

Percent change in per capita medicaid

Source: Data on state medicaid spending in fiscal years 1980 and 1994 were provided by the Center for Medicaid and State Operations in the Health Care Financing Administration. Tuition and fee increases were drawn from data from the Integrated Postsecondary Education Data System.

low tuition with the help of large state subsidies. The availability of the federal subsidies at these low tuition levels may have encouraged states facing such increasing budget demands as soaring medicaid costs to raise tuition and cut state appropriations to higher education.

Figure 3-4 shows the relationship between changes in the average tuition and required fees at public four-year institutions between 1980 and 1994 and changes in state medicaid spending per capita.[17] The states with the largest increases in this spending—New York, New Hampshire, Connecticut, Massachusetts, New Jersey, Rhode Island, and Maine—were among those with the largest increases in public four-year tuition.[18]

17. Data on state medicaid spending in fiscal years 1980 and 1994 were provided by the Center for Medicaid and State Operations in the Health Care Financing Administration.
18. The slope coefficient on the regression line shown in figure 3-2 was 4.87 with a standard error of 1.01.

This suggests that as states struggled to pay for escalating health care costs, legislatures' commitment to higher education often waned.[19]

The new tax credits for higher education included in the Taxpayer Relief Act of 1997 simply add to states' incentives to raise public tuition levels. Both the new tax credits and subsidized student loan programs absorb a share of the cost when a low-tuition institution raises tuition or cuts aid to middle-income students. For instance, the subsidized Stafford Loan program pays the interest while a student is enrolled in school. When the interest rate is 8 percent and a student borrows to pay the full amount of tuition, the in-school interest subsidy alone is equivalent to a 26 percent subsidy on the cost of freshman year tuition. However, the effect of the subsidy on the cost of a tuition increase only applies at lower tuition levels, since a student is allowed to borrow only $2,625 during the freshman year, $3,500 during the sophomore year, and $5,500 a year later under the subsidized loan program. The combination of the new tax credits and the in-school interest subsidies can function essentially as a federal cost-sharing scheme, absorbing a large share of the education expense when state legislatures raise tuition. Because the average tuition at a public two-year or four-year college is below the combined limit for student loans and the new tax credits, many state legislatures, but not private institutions that already have tuition far above the limits, are likely to be tempted by the tax credits to raise tuition.

Suppose that a state legislature cut its appropriation and raised tuition from $1,500 a year to $1,600. Considering both the loan and tax subsidies, how much would this actually cost families? Middle-income families would qualify for an additional $50 a year in tax credits during the first two years of college and $20 a year during the junior and senior years for the additional $100 in annual tuition, assuming no additional tuition increases. In order to ensure comparability, it is important to convert these figures to reflect their value at the end of four years. If the family had deposited these tax credits in an account earning 8 percent interest, they would be worth $176 at the end of four years. Similarly, if the student had not yet borrowed the maximum amount allowable under the student loan programs, he or she might qualify for an additional $87 in in-school interest subsidies while enrolled in school. In the end the $400 increase in tuition ($100 each year) would cost the family only $224 ($400 − $176) at the end of four years of college since they

19. Also see Bell (1997).

Table 3-2. *Share of Tuition Increase Paid by Families of Students and by Federal Taxpayers over a Four-Year College Career, by Initial Cost of Attendance at the Institution*[a]

Percent

Initial cost of attendance (dollars)	Federal cost sharing			Share paid by students and their families
	Hope Scholarship tax credit	Lifetime Learning tax credit	In-school interest subsidy	
0–1,000	54	9	18	19
1,000–2,000	27	9	18	46
2,000–2,625	0	9	18	73
2,625–3,500	0	9	10	80
3,500–5,000	0	9	5	86
More than 5,000	0	0	0	100

Source: Kane (1999b).

a. For simplicity, students are assumed to be eligible for the subsidized Stafford Loan program and to be borrowing to pay for tuition expenses only. In addition, the interest rate on student loans is assumed to be the same as the return available from other investments, 8 percent.

would have $176 from the tax credits to pay off the $400 increase in their loan balance. In the meantime the federal government will have lost $176 in revenue due to the tax credits and potentially paid $87 in interest through the subsidized student loan program (for a total of $263 additional dollars). Therefore, at the end of four years, families who were eligible for both the federal subsidized student loan program and the tax credits will have paid only 46 percent of the cost of a $100 hike in annual tuition, 224/(224 + 263). Federal taxpayers will have paid the remainder. (These calculations ignore any further subsidies after college, for example, in the form of below-market interest or the deductibility of student loan interest.)

Table 3-2 shows the share of any tuition increase paid for by the families of students and by federal taxpayers for institutions with different starting tuition levels. When an institution with tuition lower than $1,000 raises its tuition, the subsidy rate is even higher: 81 percent of the cost will be borne by the federal government for some families. However, by the time tuition has been raised to more than $2,625 (which exceeds the Hope Scholarship limit and the student loan limit for the student's freshman year), students and their families are paying at least 80 percent on the margin over a four-year college career.

Therefore, although the extent of implicit federal cost-sharing declines at higher tuition levels, the combination of federal programs provides a very strong incentive for low-tuition institutions to raise tuition.

As emphasized in a 1998 report by the National Commission on the Cost of Higher Education, much of the increase in public tuition during the 1980s and early 1990s was due to state legislatures' tendency to lower appropriations to public institutions, not an extraordinary rise in expenses of those institutions.[20] However, the commission's report failed to recognize that the structure of federal subsidies may have played a role by encouraging states to raise tuition by absorbing a large share of the cost when low-tuition institutions raised their charges.[21] The recent tax expenditures will simply add to that temptation. We may not have to wait long to witness the response: a number of states, including California, Louisiana, and Massachusetts, are already considering changes in their tuition and financial aid policies to take advantage of the new tax legislation.[22]

Rising Input Costs

For access to a highly trained work force, higher education must compete with other sectors of the economy. When the skills of workers become more valuable in private industry, universities have to maintain salaries or change the way they provide education. When technological innovation allows private industry to employ those resources more productively, such sectors as education in which the pace of technological innovation is more sluggish will tend to become relatively more expensive. When productivity in the general economy is increasing at 1 to 2 percent a year, real costs in industries with rigid production technologies will tend to increase 1 to 2 percent faster than inflation. Technological innovation makes labor more productive, and the sectors that innovate are willing to pay more. As the price of labor is bid up, the traditional model of lecture teaching becomes more expensive.

William Baumol and William Bowen used such an explanation to account for rising costs in fields with traditionally inflexible technolo-

20. National Commission on the Cost of Higher Education (1998).
21. McPherson, Schapiro, and Winston (1993) suggest that the inflationary effects of federal financial aid were largest in public institutions.
22. Conklin (1998).

Figure 3-5. *Nonfarm Business Productivity and the Growth of Expenditures per Student in Postsecondary Education, 1950–94*

Index (1970 = 1)

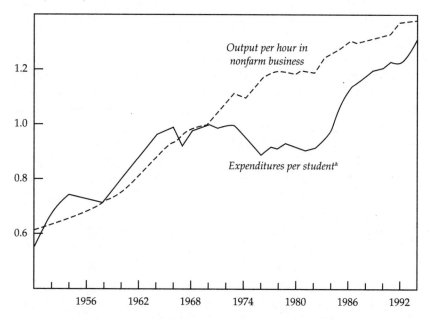

Sources: Expenditure data are from the National Center for Education Statistics (1997b, table 334, p. 350), and output data are from the Bureau of Labor Statistics.
    a. Deflated by GDP implicit price deflator.

gies, such as the performing arts and higher education.[23] In fact, the "fixed-technology—rising productivity outside of education" explanation would work pretty well in explaining the growth in expenditures per student in higher education between 1950 and 1970. Real expenditures per student in higher education (to be consistent with the productivity data, these are deflated by the GDP implicit price deflator) were rising between 1950 and 1970 at roughly the same pace as the increase in output per worker in the nonfarm business sector (figure 3-5). If the technology of education were static and if technological innovation in the remainder of the economy were raising the market value of the average workers' time, this is precisely what one might have expected.

23. Baumol and Bowen (1966).

But the simplest form of Baumol and Bowen's productivity story seems to have broken down after 1970.[24] Between 1970 and 1984, real expenditures per student in higher education remained flat, despite continued increases in productivity in the economy as a whole. Expenditures per student began rising again after 1984, but at a pace much faster than the increase in business sector productivity.

The post-1984 divergence only appears to be an anomaly, however, because productivity measures the earnings power of the *average* worker in the economy, not the workers hired by colleges and universities. Universities hire workers with very high levels of education. Yet, as is well known, the earnings of people with different levels of educational attainment diverged during the 1970s and 1980s. The average earnings of those with more than four years of college fell during the 1970s and then rose 38 percent faster than consumer prices between 1981 and 1995. Faculty salaries simply followed the market pattern set by other highly educated workers (figure 3-6).[25]

At public two-year and four-year institutions, percentage increases in educational costs per student since 1981 have been very similar to the increases in average faculty salaries (figure 3-7). As faculty salaries rose during the 1980s, college costs rose proportionately at public institutions. This is hardly surprising, since universities spend more than a third of their operating budgets on faculty salaries.[26]

Public institutions responded to increases in salaries by employing fewer faculty per full-time-equivalent student. In public two-year and four-year institutions, the number of faculty per student fell slightly between 1980 and 1995. This is precisely what one would have expected a cost-minimizing college to do—cut back on the use of factors that become more expensive.

At private four-year institutions, however, where the increases in faculty salaries and expenditures per student were larger, the response was to hire *more* faculty per student during the decade. As a result, their

24. See, for instance, Breneman (1996, pp. 57–61).

25. Postsecondary faculty and staff make up less than 6 percent of all those with postgraduate degrees in the work force. For example, 8.4 million workers reported completing five or more years of college in 1987 (in the middle of the period being considered). However, there were only 515,000 full-time instructional faculty at postsecondary institutions in 1987–88.

26. Costs of other inputs were also rising. For instance, a commonly used index of the cost of library acquisitions rose 103 percentage points faster than the consumer price index between 1980 and 1995. Halstead (1995 update, p. 30).

Figure 3-6. *Average Faculty Salary and Earnings of Male Workers with Five or More Years of College, 1971–95*

Index (1981 = 1)

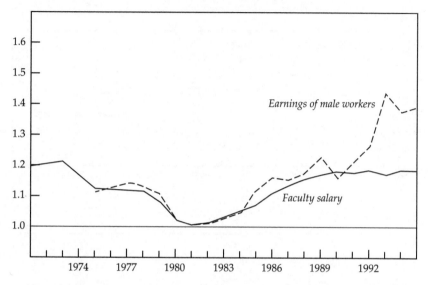

Source: Author's tabulation of data from the Integrated Postsecondary Education Data System survey and Bureau of the Census (1995, Historical Income Tables P27, P28, P28A, P28B). Both series were adjusted for inflation.

expenditures per student rose even faster than their average faculty salaries. This rapid increase in educational expenditures per student is primarily a private sector phenomenon. In a 1996 book providing a much more detailed accounting of the cost increases at four elite private institutions (Harvard University, University of Chicago, Duke University, and Carleton College), Charles Clotfelter also found that increases in input prices could account for relatively little of the rise in expenditures per student at those institutions.[27]

It might be tempting to conclude that the increased tuition at elite institutions reflects their burgeoning market power at a time of strong demand for college education. But according to Caroline Hoxby, this argument is difficult to maintain, given that the market for higher education has become increasingly competitive.[28] As transportation and

27. Clotfelter (1996).
28. Hoxby (1997).

Figure 3-7. *Postsecondary Expenditures, Faculty per Student, and Average Faculty Salary, by Type of Institution, 1971–95*

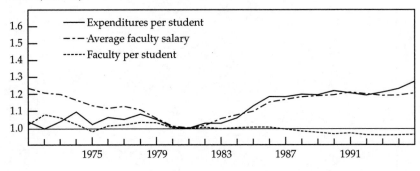

Public four-year institutions

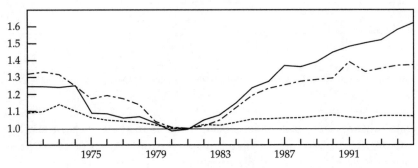

Private four-year institutions

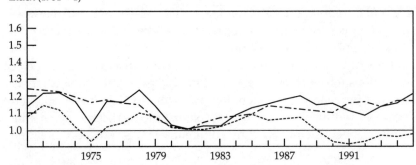

Public two-year institutions

Source: Author's calculations based on data from the Integrated Postsecondary Educational Data System.

communication costs have decreased, regional allegiances have become weaker and students have been more willing to cross state lines to attend school. Hoxby estimates that although 85 percent of college students remained in their home states in 1963, only 75 percent remained near home in 1994. The breakdown of regional allegiances was stronger in the private college market: 68 percent of private college students attended institutions in their home states in 1963, but 55 percent did so in 1994. The proportion of college freshmen reported to have applied to four or more institutions rose from 13 percent in 1980 to more than 22 percent in 1993.[29]

Possibly because many opinion makers work at highly selective Ivy League institutions, the level of selectivity in U.S. higher education is often not accurately perceived. While Harvard College may accept less than 10 percent of the students who apply, there are, in fact, very few institutions, public or private, that accept less than half their applicants. The median four-year college, public or private, denies only 25 percent of the applications it receives (table 3-3). About 9 percent of public four-year colleges and 11 percent of private four-year colleges reject more than half their applicants. Only 10 percent of private four-year colleges report that the top quarter of their freshmen class scores more than 700 on the mathematics portion of the SAT (using recentered scores), while only the top 1 percent of public four-year colleges report the same.[30] Although many college presidents would like to raise tuition unilaterally to hire an esteemed colleague from a neighboring institution or to build extravagantly appointed office space, few if any have the market power to do so without risking the loss of students.

Price Discounting in Higher Education

Elite private institutions not only became more expensive, they also began charging a wider range of prices.[31] Anyone hoping to interpret their pricing and admissions decisions using the usual profit-maximization framework is bound to be perplexed. On the one hand, financial aid officers occasionally set prices in a way that would make even a Microsoft executive blush. A 1996 story in the *Wall Street Journal* reported how at least one institution provided less aid to students

29. Astin, Korn, and Riggs (1993, p. 3).

30. On the recentered SAT test, 700 is approximately the 95th percentile. College Board (1997).

31. Much of the discussion in this section appeared in Kane (1999a).

Table 3-3. *Private and Public Four-Year College Selectivity, by Measure, 1996–97*

Percentile (weighted by enrollment)	Percent of applications denied	SAT math score (top 25 percent)	SAT verbal score (top 25 percent)	Percent of freshmen with high school GPAs greater than 3.0
		Private four-year colleges		
Bottom 1	3.4	480	510	12
5th	8.6	520	530	20
10th	10.9	540	560	26
25th	16.1	580	590	49
Median	25.2	620	620	69
75th	37.5	660	670	85
90th	59.2	720	710	96
95th	69.3	740	740	98
Top 1	81.2	770	780	100
		Public four-year colleges		
Bottom 1	1.3	500	490	12
5th	7.0	520	520	23
10th	11.1	530	530	33
25th	16.5	560	560	54
Median	25.1	600	600	70
75th	34.9	630	630	85
90th	46.0	660	660	96
95th	55.9	670	670	98
Top 1	65.3	700	700	100

Source: Author's calculations based on College Board 1996–97 Annual Survey of Colleges.

traveling long distances to visit campus, using such behavior as a measure of a student's attachment to the school and exacting the appropriate toll.[32] On the other hand, these same institutions regularly turn away thousands of applicants willing to pay the full price, while offering generous financial aid packages to low-income students.

Why would the same college go out of its way to capture additional tuition revenue from one group of students, yet forgo many more thousands of dollars from wealthy applicants that could be accepted? Col-

---

32. Steve Stecklow, "Expensive Lesson: Colleges Manipulate Financial Aid Offers, Shortchanging Many," *Wall Street Journal*, April 1, 1996, p. A1.

leges differ from the typical economic decisionmaker in two fundamental ways. First, students are not only customers, but contributors in the educational process.[33] They learn from each other in the classroom, study groups, and dormitory rooms. This is reflected in the pages of college guidebooks, which are filled with detailed information on the characteristics of the student body but offer comparatively little information on the stature and publication record of an institution's faculty. Students matter not only because their tuition dollars keep a college afloat, but because they do much of the teaching (and, I can say from personal experience, not all of the learning). The characteristics of classmates may be valuable because, in a labor market where it is difficult for any employer to observe directly an employee's ability, the general reputation of the college a student attended may serve as a badge of honor, especially early in someone's career.

Therefore, the true cost of educating students with academic preparation better than the average is actually less than the cost of bricks and mortar and faculty time required to teach them because of the value they add to the education of their classmates. For precisely the opposite reason, the net cost of educating students below the mean is probably greater than the more easily measured costs of bricks and mortar because of the costs they impose on the reputation of the school. Even a college with little market power would take such cost differences for different types of students into account.

The second way the usual model of producer price setting does not fit colleges' financial aid decisions is that many also think of themselves as charitable foundations, dispensing the gifts bequeathed by earlier generations (either in the form of endowment income or scenic campuses) to further other social goals—greater racial understanding or socioeconomic mobility or aesthetic pursuits.

In a 1998 book, Elizabeth Duffy and Idana Goldberg describe the recurring battles fought over the appropriate mix between need-based financial aid and "merit-based" aid distributed according to any other criterion, such as athletic ability, test scores, or an interest in renaissance literature.[34] For those who believe that every dollar spent on merit aid is one dollar less for need-based aid, this is more than a strategic decision. It is a battle between right and wrong.

33. Rothschild and White (1995); Winston (1999).
34. Duffy and Goldberg (1998).

Yet the trade-off between a dollar in merit-based aid or a dollar in need-based aid is probably not one-for-one.[35] Because a college's customers are also contributors to their classmates' education, academic scholarships for academically talented students are often a substitute for a new coat of paint on dormitory windows or salaries for additional assistant professors as a means for improving a college's product.[36] On many campuses, one dollar more for merit aid may mean one dollar less for faculty fringe benefits or for journal subscriptions, rather than any reduction in the need-based financial aid budget. Such operational decisions about the least costly method for improving a school's product are certainly debatable, but they hardly rise to the level of a moral wrong. On the contrary, one might argue that in today's competitive environment, tying a school's hands and ruling out merit aid may lead to an unethical waste of an institution's resources on less effective means for producing educational value (such as raising senior faculty salaries).

Merit aid is often the only prudent response to a more competitive environment of college applicants.[37] As students apply to a wider range of institutions, all but a handful of colleges have become price takers rather than price setters. Differences in financial aid packages more closely resemble differences in the value that applicants bring to the institution. For any school with a mean SAT test score of 1,100, there is an increasingly uniform maximum price that a student with a SAT of 1,400 would be willing to pay, regardless of need. If a college hoped to charge more, there are likely to be many other institutions of similar levels of selectivity willing to attract the student with a more generous offer. In many industries, differing prices for different buyers of the same product are taken as a sign of market power. However, in higher education, such price discrimination is a result of the *declining* market power of colleges. Competition tends to force an institution's prices closer to its costs. But because each student adds a different amount to the value of his or her classmates' degrees, the net cost of educating

35. Baum (1998) makes a similar point.

36. Earlier in this chapter, I argued that one should exclude scholarship and fellowship expenditures when measuring the educational cost. The argument here would suggest that some portion of scholarship and fellowship expenditures also represents a cost of an input. However, because it is not possible to determine how much of scholarships and fellowships represent a "cost," I continue to exclude them.

37. Hoxby (1997).

each student is different even if the cost of the bricks and mortar is similar.

The increasing payoff to elite education in the labor market and the proliferation of college rankings (which rely heavily on more readily measured indicators such as a college's mean SAT score) may have contributed to this widening dispersion of prices charged for different students. A college's reputation used to be built on an amorphous mix of perceived selectivity, quality of the faculty, and the square footage of the library—in which the average characteristics of the students undoubtedly played a part—but the high visibility of national rankings implies that the marginal impact of any change in a school's student body from year to year has almost certainly increased. As a result, its least talented students cost a college more and its most talented students cost a college less than they used to, even if nothing else has changed.

Within the constraints imposed by the alternative options of their applicants, colleges are still free to use their wealth to provide additional financial aid to low-income students. Markets may increasingly determine the maximum that a student with a given level of preparation would expect to pay at a given type of institution, but this does not prevent colleges from charging less. However, rather than being drawn out of "excess profits" gleaned from middle- and higher-income parents, these resources are probably more accurately thought of as being drawn from the endowment, because in such a competitive market, there may be few excess resources to be had.

However, the rationale for merit aid offered by institutions is quite different from that for publicly funded merit aid programs such as Georgia's Hope Scholarship program. Suppose a particularly talented youth were planning to attend Georgia Tech instead of Emory University in Atlanta. If the youth offered a particularly valuable set of talents, Emory might offer a $3,000 scholarship to lure the student to their campus. If the youth accepted the offer, the youth and the other students at Emory would both, presumably, benefit. Moreover, their gain must have exceeded Georgia Tech's loss or, we could safely presume, Georgia Tech would have responded. In this instance, the use of merit aid has led to an improvement in social welfare.

However, suppose that the state of Georgia offered the student a scholarship worth $3,000 if he or she attended any college within the state of Georgia. Because this second form of "merit aid" does not change the relative price of the two choices, the student would presumably choose to attend where he or she was planning to attend anyway—Georgia Tech. The student's family is $3,000 better off and the taxpayers of Georgia are $3,000 worse off, but nothing else has changed. Merit aid that does not encourage a student to do anything other than what they were otherwise planning to do is simply a transfer, and there is no gain in welfare as a result. Any hopes of benefits for the taxpayers of Georgia rest on persuading some youth to remain in state who would have attended elsewhere instead, and the subsequent hope that they may be more likely to remain in Georgia after graduation.

The more problematic question is whether colleges are justified in using the information in a student's file to offer less generous financial aid to those with stronger emotional attachments as signaled by campus visits, early admission applications, and so forth—the practices described in the *Wall Street Journal* article. One might think of a particularly scenic campus or the emotional attachments of the children of alumni as being part of an institution's endowment. Using such attachments to fund need-based financial aid is in many ways analogous to investing the financial portion of a university's endowment wisely to be able to pursue its other goals. Indeed, some might argue that institutions bear a fiduciary responsibility to get the highest return out of their full endowment, not just the portion that is invested in financial instruments, and use whatever information they can to stretch the university's financial aid budget.

In *The Student Aid Game* Michael McPherson and Martin Schapiro advocate federal policies of subsidizing greater use of need-based aid by institutions.[38] There may also be good news for advocates of need-based aid in the increasingly competitive market. The same market conditions that force university leaders to consider merit aid also provide them with additional leverage in their pursuit of larger social goals. Because most schools place some value on the socioeconomic diversity of their student body, an additional dollar spent on need-based financial aid at one institution may encourage peer institutions to do the same. The chain reaction to the decision by the trustees at Princeton to provide $2 million more financial aid to middle-income students is evidence of such a phenomenon. If the annual costs of the Harvard, Stanford, and Yale initiatives announced in response to the

38. McPherson and Schapiro (1998).

Princeton reforms were combined, the increases in need-based aid would be more than eight times larger ($16.8 million versus $2 million spent by Princeton).[39] Therefore, the proliferation of competition has also increased the multiplier effects of any one college's altruistic decisions.

Duffy and Goldberg have reported that the rise in applications during the late 1960s and early 1970s led many private colleges to expand enrollments.[40] But the authors leave unanswered why elite institutions did not similarly expand when they were flooded with applications during the 1980s. The answer may be that during the 1970s, as the pay-off to college was falling (as noted by Richard Freeman in *The Overeducated American*), it was much less costly to admit additional students who otherwise might not have been accepted, since any decline in standards resulting from expanded admission was less costly than before.[41] However, during the 1980s the payoff to skill seemed to jump.[42] Caroline Hoxby and Bridget Long, as well as Dominic Brewer, Eric Eide, and Ronald Ehrenberg reported some evidence that the payoff to attending an elite institution also rose, even after controlling for the higher test scores of the students attending them.[43] Therefore, during the 1980s, any expansion in admission standards that led to a deterioration in the average characteristics of the student body would have been more costly to the value of a student's degree than before. As the value of the average characteristics of the school rose, the cost of admitting the least qualified student would have been rising because the penalties imposed on other students by his or her admission would be increasing.

McPherson and Schapiro noted in 1998 that the amount of aid not based on need that was given to incoming freshmen roughly tripled at both public and private four-year colleges between 1983–84 and 1991–92 (although private colleges continued to give out three times as much non-need-based aid as public institutions).[44] Because test scores

---

39. McPherson and Shapiro (1998); "Worth the Wait: Harvard's New Financial Aid Program Leads the League," *Harvard Crimson*, September 17, 1998; "Details of 3 New Student Aid Plans," *Chronicle of Higher Education*, March 6, 1998, p. A43.
40. Duffy and Goldberg (1998).
41. Freeman (1976).
42. Murnane, Willett, and Levy (1995).
43. Brewer, Eide, and Ehrenberg (1996); Hoxby and Long (1999).
44. McPherson and Schapiro (1998, table 11.1).

and high school performance are also positively related to family income, the increasing reliance on non-need-based aid is often thought of as a net loss for low-income students, drawing funds away from the aid programs colleges focus specifically on them. But the net effect of non-need-based scholarships and fellowships is unclear once one recognizes that students are contributors to the educational process as well as customers. Luring academically talented youth to attend one's school may simply be a cheaper way than alternative strategies to produce a higher-quality education. To the extent that colleges have been increasingly using financial aid to attract abler students rather than hiring additional faculty, they may simply be minimizing costs, not giving away resources that would have gone to low-income students.

Conclusion

A 1998 *New York Times* story about costs in higher education, "The Ivory Tower under Siege," reflected the public's anxiety about increasing tuition with its provocative subtitle, "Everyone Else Has Downsized, Why Not the Academy?"[45] Although the question seems like a simple one, the answer, as usual, is more complicated.

Rather than a single, uniform increase in cost and tuition, there are four distinct trends to be explained and, it seems, four different explanations to account for them. First, a large share of the rise in tuition charges at public institutions was not due to a change in the underlying costs per student on campus but to a decline in the share of costs covered by state and local appropriations. As the fiscal demands placed upon state medicaid and correctional budgets grew, state legislatures were paying a decreasing share of the costs at public institutions. Even if college presidents had succeeded in holding cost increases to the rate of inflation, tuition would have risen by roughly two-thirds simply because of this shift in state fiscal priorities.

Second, to the extent that costs per student did increase, the increases were largely in line with changes in the wages of more educated workers in the economy—at public institutions, at least. During the 1980s,

45. William Honan, "The Ivory Tower under Siege: Everyone Else Has Downsized, Why Not the Academy?" *New York Times,* January 4, 1998.

the most educated workers in America, those with graduate degrees, were one of the only groups of American workers whose incomes were rising considerably more rapidly than the rate of inflation. Reflecting this larger trend, faculty salaries did rise by roughly a third from 1980. Given that universities depend on a highly educated work force to deliver their services, expenditures per student also rose at public two-year and four-year colleges, albeit less dramatically than tuition.

Third, expenditures per pupil rose more dramatically at private institutions. Moreover, unlike public institutions, which hired fewer faculty per student in response to rising faculty salaries, private institutions actually began hiring *more* faculty per student, despite the increase in cost. Such statistics fuel the fire of parental resentment of faculty greed. But a simple story of greed seems unlikely. The increase in expenditures was not limited to the highly selective institutions, which were arguably more insulated from competition. Because the rise in private college expenditures per student occured even in those sectors where competition is fierce, it is unlikely that the increase was based simply on the greed, or sloth, or inflexibility of private college faculties.

Moreover, at the price levels where parents and students were bargaining with private colleges, there are few federal financial aid subsidies to be blamed for the increase. When a private four-year college raises tuition from, say, $10,000 to $10,500, a student's family—not federal taxpayers—can expect to pay the lion's share of the increase. The reason is that the federal subsidized loan and grant programs are subject to limits that are generally less than $5,500. Both tuition and expenditures per student have risen dramatically at private institutions, but federal financial aid programs are an unlikely candidate for blame.

Finally, the increasing proclivity of colleges to charge different prices for different students also is probably not evidence of colleges aggressively exercising market power, but just the opposite: the increasingly competitive market for more talented students means that colleges find it even more difficult to charge a uniform price. Given the emphasis placed by college rankings on readily measurable student body characteristics, such as test scores, colleges have to worry more than ever about the message their admissions decisions one year send to the prospective class for next year. Because of their impact on these statistics, the most talented student admitted contributes more and the least talented student admitted costs more. To some extent, colleges' pricing decisions have reflected this harsh reality.

Participants in the popular discussion sometimes argue that the rise in tuition charges may reflect a desire by private colleges to signal exclusivity, as if high tuition were the primary way in which colleges can signal quality. However, while this may be an explanation for a rise in average sticker prices, it is quite unlikely to explain the rise in the actual price, net of financial aid. As long as it is difficult for any student to observe all other students' aid packages, colleges could simply raise tuition and financial aid packages simultaneously to send an empty signal of improved quality. But it would be hard for them to get away with raising the average net price with this strategy. If a college did not raise grants for students by the same amount as the sticker price, its competitors could simply match the sticker price hike and offer more aid to capture its students.

There are a number of other ways in which colleges can signal their exclusivity without using price: building a new student union building, hiring a Nobel prize winner, attracting more star students. While all of these cost money, they are easily signaled, and as a result, colleges may be able to charge their students more for them. Although the Rolls Royce and Mercedes Benz models are still available, casual observation of the new car market suggests that there is a wider selection of expensive sport utility vehicles and luxury sedans than there was fifteen years ago. While the Mercedes Benzes and Rolls Royces of the higher education market are still out there, there are probably more Lexuses and Infinitis in higher education too.

I do not mean to imply that colleges could not do more to rein in costs. Nor do I mean to dismiss the possibility that common institutional rigidities have hampered cost-cutting efforts across higher education. However, unlike health care, where traditional fee-for-service financing contributed to the rise in costs during the 1980s, one would be hard-pressed to find a cause in the financing system for higher education.

On the contrary, the federal financial aid programs have largely preserved college administrators' and faculties' incentives to keep costs down. Because the federal subsidies are largely irrelevant at the price levels currently being charged, each dollar in cost savings that a college finds is not forfeited in the form of lost federal aid, but could potentially be used to pursue other goals—to hire an esteemed colleague, to attract a star student, to provide an opportunity to another low-income student. While faculty senate charters and professorial tenure may make it difficult for universities to find those opportunities, one would be mistaken to blame the financing structure for the problems universities face in reining in costs.

4

Has Financial Aid Policy Succeeded in Ensuring Access to College?

In the past two decades the debate over the reauthorization of the Higher Education Act and over postsecondary financial aid policy in general has devolved into a crude scramble for spoils in which public and private college associations, student associations, and banks seek to protect their constituents' narrow interests. Private banks and guarantee agencies and the representatives of private colleges, state universities, community colleges, and even for-profit training institutions employ their own experts, knowledgeable regarding the arcane details of financial aid program rules, to do combat over the bounty. Now and then changes in critical congressional committee chairmanships or some other force upsets the equilibrium, setting off a new scramble for resources. But even at these times, there is rarely a lucid discussion of the conflicting goals of financial aid policies or the success or failure of existing policies in achieving them.

The strongest evidence for the lack of direction is the absence of any effort to define and measure progress in meeting the programs' goals. The federal government spends over $6 billion a year on the Pell Grant program, but the Department of Education has never attempted to evaluate the program's impact on the college enrollment of low-income people. The department publishes reams of statistics on who receives Pell Grants, the proportion of grant spending received by various types of postsecondary institutions, and the geographic distribution of spending. But there is no information on the net effect on enrollment rates of various groups or on tuition charges of individual institutions. The limits of data collection largely reflect the limits of the current debate, which is confined to how the pie is to be divided rather than focused on the goals of financial aid policy.

One might expect that one goal would be to increase the college enrollments of low-income youth. But nowhere does the federal statistical system regularly monitor college enrollment by family income from one year to the next.[1] In fact, not until 1987 did the Department of Education begin collecting data on the financial aid received by individual students from various sources, allowing researchers and policymakers to observe how the various programs of federal, state, local, and institutional aid interact.

The basic framework of the financial aid system—the federal grant and loan programs, the need-analysis system, campus-based programs—has been in place since the mid-1970s. And since then federal policy has been limited to making minor changes in existing programs. A fruitful discussion of potential structural reforms requires reexamining the original policy goals. This chapter lays the groundwork for that discussion.

Rationales for Public Action

Many believe there is social value—altruism, civic conscience, commitment to civil liberties—generated by schooling that is not captured by students or their families as either intellectual enjoyment or higher earnings. To the extent such value exists, people pursuing their self-interest are likely to underinvest in education, or at least in the types of education that produce social value. Ernest Pascarella and Patrick Terenzini have summarized studies on the influence of college education on these noneconomic outcomes.[2] After attempting to control for differences between college-bound graduates and other high school graduates, much of the research suggests that higher education has a beneficial influence on civic-minded values, building the social capital of the nation.

---

1. The department has collected surveys following the graduates of the high school classes of 1972, 1980, 1982, and 1992. However, changes over time in the manner of collection of family income makes even such long-term comparisons difficult. In recent years the National Center for Education Statistics has begun including a series collected by the Census Bureau with information on college enrollment by household income. But because parental income information is not reported for college students who form their own households, it is not possible to trace college enrollment rates by family income. See Kane (1997).

2. Pascarella and Terenzini (1991).

Whether these effects are real, or even whether they are worth the price taxpayers are paying, are matters of debate. It is often argued that such social products of educational attainment as basic literacy are produced during primary and secondary education, and postsecondary training produces mostly private benefits, not public ones. I will not rehash the arguments here.

This chapter will focus instead on the effects of financial aid policies in relieving the economic constraints on the investment decisions of low-income families. This is not because I think the social value of education is unimportant—indeed, I have spent much of my life in academic research and teaching because I believe it is very important. Rather, I do not dwell on it because I have little to add to the argument. The nature of the evidence is admittedly soft, offering little leverage to move the debate forward. Any lever with the potential to overcome the inertia must rest on a surface strong enough to be recognized by the other members of the debate. The current state of knowledge, and probable future knowledge, of the social benefits is unlikely to be sufficiently firm to serve that purpose because the outcomes are so hard to measure and the incremental benefits so difficult to estimate.

Economic Development and the Rising Payoffs of College Education

During the 1980s, the gap in earnings between people with postsecondary training and other high school graduates widened. Although it might be easier to justify a larger total investment in postsecondary education on the basis of such labor market evidence, it is hard to justify greater *public* investment. Families who are paying attention to the labor market can see for themselves the increased importance of postsecondary training. Indeed, very soon after the gap in earnings began to widen in the early 1980s, college enrollment rates began to increase (see figure 1-1). In fact, enrollment rates started to rise even before the change in labor market conditions was widely noted by professional labor economists.

If there is an economic rationale for public intervention in higher education, it is to ensure that all families have access to the resources to finance worthwhile investments on their own. But economists have long recognized that private capital markets are likely to underinvest in human capital because students are barred from offering their future economic capabilities as collateral to private lenders. To borrow Gary

Becker's sardonic phrase, "courts have frowned on contracts that even indirectly suggest involuntary servitude."[3] Without collateral, even students with promising careers may have difficulty obtaining private financing. Although young people from high-income families may be able to secure financing from their parents, those from low-income families cannot.

To remedy this market imperfection, societies have invented a variety of mechanisms—direct subsidies to institutions, means-tested voucher programs for low-income students, federally guaranteed loan programs—for channeling the resources to students and families when it comes time to invest in college. The federal government provides $8 billion a year in means-tested grant and work study aid to low-income college students and $33 billion a year in federally guaranteed education loans.[4] State and local governments provide $49 billion a year in appropriations to public institutions and $3.3 billion in means-tested grant aid. Have these sizable public subsidies eliminated the constraints on college investment by low-income youth?

As discussed in chapter 2, there is a considerable amount of aid already available. Grant aid actually exceeded tuition charges at public two-year and four-year colleges for the average full-time student from a family with income less than $20,000 (see table 2-2). Although the average student from a family with income less than $10,000 attending a public two-year college full time paid about $902 in tuition in 1992–93, he or she also received $848 in federal grant aid (primary Pell Grants) and $328 in state and other grant aid to offset the costs, meaning that the net tuition paid was a *negative* $279. The same was true at public four-year institutions. And low-income students attending private four-year institutions paid only slightly more than $3,000 to attend full time, far less than the $12,078 paid by the average student with family income greater than $100,000.

Given the large amounts of grant aid received by low-income students attending college, one might be tempted to conclude that financial constraints could not be an important problem in rationing access to college. However, financial aid statistics provide an incomplete picture of potential barriers to attendance by low-income youth. First, these

3. Becker (1993, p. 93).
4. The student aid figures are drawn from College Board (1998, table 2). The evidence on state and local appropriations is drawn from the National Center for Education Statistics (1998, table 329, p. 353).

young people are paying far larger costs than the tuition bills. The average income of an 18- to 24-year-old male high school graduate working full time in 1992 was $16,900. If a student were to forgo nine months of this salary to attend college full-time, his costs would amount to $12,675, which greatly exceeds the tuition costs at the average public two-year or four-year college. Therefore, it is not just tuition costs that families face, but the cost of forgone earnings as well.

Conventional wisdom suggests that a tuition bill may put more strain on a family's resources than forgone earnings because tuition is a "real" cost and future earnings a "hypothetical" one. But as Becker has observed, for a person with other bills to pay, forgone earnings and tuition are equivalent.[5] For instance, for a person facing a $15,000 cost of supporting a family, it makes no difference whether one is forgoing $12,000 in earnings and receiving free tuition or paying $12,000 in tuition with no opportunity costs. Either way, the family's current cash position is $12,000 less than it would have been without entering school, and the person must still finance the family's housing, food, clothing, and so on.[6]

Despite the availability of student loans described in chapter 2, the federal programs are not a complete solution to all families' financing needs. And borrowing under the federal student loan programs has always been subject to annual limits (table 4-1). For instance, between 1976 and 1985 the annual borrowing limit for a student was fixed in nominal dollars at $2,500, despite substantial increases in both the real and nominal tuitions. Since 1992 the most a student could borrow under the Stafford Loan program has been $2,625 during the freshman year, $3,500 during the sophomore year, and $5,500 a year thereafter. Some students receive additional loans through the Perkins Loan program, but Perkins is not an entitlement program and funds are limited. Independent students—those who are married, have dependents, are veterans, or are older than 24—can borrow an additional $4,000 a year during the first two years and an additional $5,000 a year thereafter. Beginning in 1993, parents were allowed to borrow up to the full cost of attendance under the PLUS program. But since payments on these loans begin immediately, such loans will be of little use to those with liquidity problems.

5. Becker (1993).
6. For more on the theory of education investments in the presence of financing constraints, see Jacoby (1991) and Wallace and Ihnen (1975).

Table 4-1. *Federal Loan Programs for College Undergraduates, by Characteristics, Selected Years, 1976–92*

	Student loan programs			Parent loans, supplemental student loans
Year	Loan limits (current dollars)	Interest rates	Income restrictions (current dollars)	
1976	$2,500 a year ($7,500 aggregate limit)	7% (fixed)	In-school subsidy if income less than $25,000	None
1978	$2,500 a year	7% (fixed)	No needs test	None
1981	$2,500 a year ($12,500 aggregate limit)	9% (fixed)	Needs test required for incomes greater than $30,000	PLUS program: parents can borrow additional $3,000 at 9% interest rate
1983	As 1981	8% (fixed)	As 1981	PLUS program: parents can borrow additional $3,000
1984	As 1981	As 1983	As 1981	PLUS program: parents can borrow additional $4,000 at 12%
1986	$2,625 a year (years 1 and 2), $4,000 a year (years 3 and on) ($17,250 aggregate limit)	8% for years 1–4 of repayment; 10% for remainder of loan	All students must demonstrate financial need	PLUS program: parents can borrow $4,000 a year at 3-month T-bill plus 3.5% ($20,000 aggregate limit); SLS program: up to $4,000 a year ($20,000 aggregate limit)
1992	$2,625 (year 1), $3,500 (year 2), $5,500 a year afterward ($23,00 aggregate limit)	Variable rate of T-bill + 3.1% with a cap of 9%	As 1986	PLUS program: parents can borrow up to the full cost of attendance at one-year T-bill plus 3.1% with a cap of 10%; SLS program: $4,000 (years 1 and 2), $5,000 a year afterward at one-year T-bill + 3.1% with a cap of 11%
1993	As 1992	Cap of 8.25%	As 1992	Establish direct loan, unsubsidized loan programs
1998	As 1992	Variable rate of T-bill + 2.3% with a cap of 8.25%	As 1992	As 1993

Source: U.S. Department of Education (various years).

Figure 4-1. *Distribution of Federal Loans to College Undergraduates, 1992–93*

Percent

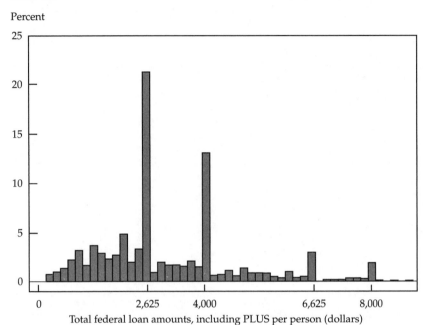

Total federal loan amounts, including PLUS per person (dollars)

Source: Author's tabulation of data from the National Postsecondary Student Aid Study, 1992–93.

Figure 4-1 shows the distribution of total student and parent borrowing under the federal programs during the 1992–93 academic year, when first- or second-year dependent students were limited to $2,625 in borrowing under the Stafford Loan program and upper-level undergraduates could borrow up to $4,000 a year. Independent students could borrow $4,000 extra a year under the Supplemental Loans to Students program. More than a third of borrowers under the student loan programs were stacked up at either $2,625 or $4,000. The distribution also had spikes at $6,625 and $8,000, the limits for independent students.[7] It is clear that the limits are binding for many families.

7. National Center for Education Statistics (1995, pp. 68, 80, 90). Many of the students between these spikes may also have been constrained because they could not borrow more than the cost of attendance minus their expected family contribution. Some states and institutions have their own loan programs. However, in the 1992–93 school year, less than 1 percent of undergraduates received either a state loan (0.4 percent) or an institutional loan (0.5 percent). In contrast, 19 percent of undergraduates received federal loans.

But borrowing limits are not the only constraints on families' ability to finance a college education. There may be substantial costs of simply learning what types of aid are available. Gary Orfield cited several studies suggesting that low-income families are often unaware of eligibility rules and procedures.[8]

The problem is not just that many families are unaware of available programs, but also that they may be deterred from applying. For those who itemize their taxes, the financial aid form may be less complicated than a tax form; but for those who do not itemize, the application form is likely to be *more* vexing. One reason is that it asks families to report not only the income from assets but the value of the assets themselves. The nonmonetary "hassle" costs of such paperwork may be particularly large for low-income, potential first-generation college students undecided or hesitant about enrolling.

Fairness and efficiency sometimes justify imposing such costs on applicants to ensure that resources are being received by the intended beneficiaries.[9] For example, waiting in line to apply for unemployment benefits is more costly for those with higher opportunity costs and as a result may serve as a useful rationing device to screen out those with better employment options. But in the case of financial aid, compliance costs may actually be greater for low-income youth whom society would most like to affect. Therefore, the complicated process of applying for aid may actually reduce target efficiency rather than improve it.

The existing financial aid system is an incomplete solution to overcoming financing constraints in the market for people with higher education. The rest of the chapter evaluates just how much any remaining constraints may limit the choice of low-income youth.

Financial Constraints and College Investment Decisions

It is impossible to evaluate how much public subsidies have eased the financial problems of attending college by simply asking families whether they can "afford" college. Parents and students may claim to be unable to pay for college for a number of reasons, only some of which would be related to financing. In addition, people tend to rationalize their behavior after the fact, even if the actual cause was very

8. Orfield (1992).
9. Nichols and Zeckhauser (1982).

different. Instead of direct survey questions, one has to rely on indirect evidence to evaluate the importance of financing constraints in families' decisionmaking.

In the sections that follow, I evaluate four types of evidence of constrained behavior by college students. First, I examine differences in college enrollment among high- and low-income youth with similar academic preparation when they graduate from high school. Then I evaluate the price sensitivity of youth to variations in college cost, paying particular attention to sensitivity to variations in tuition. Next I examine the relation of tuition sensitivity and responsiveness to increases during the 1980s in the payoffs to schooling. Finally, I look at the potential importance of the lack of information on people considering college entry. Although each piece of evidence is indirect, all suggest that significant barriers remain, preventing families from investing in college education based solely on the educational merits of the decision.

Differences in College Entry by Family Income

A first test of the importance of financing constraints is to study differences in college enrollment for young people from high- and low-income families. To do so, I employed data from the National Education Longitudinal Study of 1988, a panel study of the eighth grade cohort of 1988, which was surveyed at two-year intervals between 1988 and 1994. The 1994 questionnaire asked the participants to report postsecondary enrollment between 1992 and 1994. A person who reported any enrollment—part time or full time—at a community college, four-year college, proprietary school, or public technical institute between June 1992 and August 1994 was considered to have enrolled. Only those responding in the base year and the three follow-ups who reported a high school diploma or Graduate Equivalency Diploma by 1994 were included in the analysis. The family income measure was reported by parents when students were in the eighth grade.[10]

The first column of table 4-2 shows the differences in the proportion of respondents reporting postsecondary enrollment by family income quintile and ethnicity. (The excluded category includes white non-Hispanic youth from families from the lowest income quintile.) The differences

10. Although the family income measure is categorical, income categories were combined to correspond as closely as possible to quintiles.

Table 4-2. *Eighth Grade Cohort of 1988 Differences in Likelihood of Reporting Postsecondary Training by 1994, by Family Background and Test Scores*[a]

| Characteristic | Ordinary least squares | | | | | Two-stage least squares |
	(1)	(2)	(3)	(4)	(5)	(6)
Black,	.022	.107	.091	.097	.095	.099
non-Hispanic	(.018)	(.018)	(.018)	(.017)	(.018)	(.018)
Hispanic	.054	.101	.105	.104	.082	.105
	(.015)	(.014)	(.015)	(.015)	(.016)	(.015)
Other,	.098	.055	.077	.042	.024	.047
non-Hispanic	(.017)	(.017)	(.017)	(.017)	(.016)	(.017)
Family income quintile						
4th	.109	.075	.085	.061	.064	.060
	(.018)	(.017)	(.018)	(.018)	(.018)	(.018)
3d	.167	.113	.125	.091	.093	.089
	(.018)	(.017)	(.018)	(.018)	(.018)	(.018)
2d	.242	.159	.179	.122	.123	.121
	(.017)	(.017)	(.017)	(.018)	(.018)	(.018)
Top	.338	.211	.236	.150	.146	.150
	(.017)	(.016)	(.016)	(.018)	(.018)	(.018)
Highest parental education						
High school	...	...	...	.039	.036	.038
dropout	...	...	...	(.023)	(.023)	(.023)
Some college	...	...	...	.104	.103	.103
	...	...	...	(.014)	(.014)	(.014)
Undergraduate	...	...	...	.164	.161	.161
degree	...	...	...	(.015)	(.015)	(.015)
Postgraduate	...	...	...	.156	.156	.152
degree	...	...	...	(.015)	(.015)	(.016)
1992 test scores	No	Yes	No	Yes	Yes	Yes
1988 test scores	No	No	Yes	No	No	IV for '92 score
State dummies	No	No	No	No	Yes	No
p-value on H_0: family income differential = 0	.000	.000	.000	.000	.000	.000

Source: Author's calculations based on the National Education Longitudinal Study of 1988.

a. The results were estimated with a linear probability specification. Huber-White standard errors in parentheses allow for arbitrary correlation across individuals attending the same high schools. The mean postsecondary entry rate for the sample of 7,820 is 77.1 percent. The test scores were the standardized tests in reading and math available for the NELS sample.

between young people from poor families and those from wealthier ones in the proportion receiving postsecondary training are very large. The average person from the fourth-highest quintile of family income was 11 percentage points more likely to report some postsecondary training than a person in the bottom quintile; those in the top quintile were 34 percentage points more likely to enroll.[11] These differences were very large given that the predicted postsecondary entry rate for someone with average characteristics was 77 percent.

College enrollment apparently differs dramatically by family income, but so do students' levels of preparation for college. As a result, differences in college attendance by family income reflect longer-term differences in high- and low-income families' investments in educational attainment. Higher-income parents are more likely to have sent their children to private schools or may have purchased homes in neighborhoods with more effective public schools. But because the financial return to postsecondary education may well differ for those with different levels of academic preparation, one might want to distinguish between the relationship between family income and college enrollment in the full sample and the relationship observed for students emerging from high school with similar levels of academic preparation.

Therefore, the second column of table 4-2 reports the difference in postsecondary enrollment by race and income, *after* including students' math and reading test scores in 1992 as crude measures of differences in academic preparation at the end of high school. Those in the fourth-lowest quintile of family income were still 8 percentage points more likely to enter postsecondary schooling than those from the lowest-income quintile, who also had the mean test scores and racial makeup in the sample. The differential also remained large (21 percentage points) between the top and bottom quintile.

To the extent that those not headed to college because of family financial limitations also work less hard in high school in anticipation of their being unable to attend college, the estimates in column 2 may overcompensate for preexisting differences in the human capital of high- and low-income youth. As a result, column 3 reports similar results after taking account of test scores from 1988, when the students would

11. Interestingly, black and Hispanic youth seemed to be slightly more likely than white, non-Hispanic youth of similar income to have reported some college enrollment.

have been in eighth grade. The differentials in postsecondary enroll-ment by family income are slightly larger, using test scores from 1988 rather than scores from 1992 to control for preexisting differences in the stock of human capital. In other words, a small part of the difference may have been due to differences in academic progress in high school, but the differences are not great.

Column 4 adds indicators of highest parental educational attainment to the specification. To the extent that differences in college entry among the children of the more and less educated reflect differences in the importance attached to education, one might want to take account of dif-ferences in parental education when looking for evidence of financial constraints. But variation in parental education among those with similar current levels of income may simply reflect longer-term differences in family wealth and therefore may partly reflect differences in families' ability to self-finance college. Therefore, the relationship between college enrollment and family income without controlling for parental education may overstate the importance of family income, while the relationship among those with similar parental education may underestimate the importance of family access to capital. Table 4-2 reports both.

The differences in college enrollment by family income, reported in column 4, remained large even after including indicators of parental education in the specification: a 6 percentage point difference between the bottom two family income quintiles after holding constant both parental education and test scores, and a 15 percentage point difference between youth in the top and bottom family income groups.

As reported in column 5, none of the results are affected by including state dummies to capture correlations between state and regional dif-ferences in college enrollment rates and family income, race, and parental education.

To gauge the possible effects of mismeasurement of academic prepa-ration in the 1992 standardized test scores, column 6 reports the results of instrumenting for the 1992 test scores with the 1988 test scores.[12] Differences in postsecondary entry by family income were largely unaffected.

12. To the extent that 1988 test scores may have their own independent positive effect on postsecondary enrollment, these results may overstate the importance of twelfth-grade test scores in predicting college enrollment and therefore understate the family income differences.

Differences by Income and Test Score Quartile

Table 4-3 reports differentials in postsecondary entry estimated separately for students in each mathematics test score quartile in 1992, with and without controls for measures of parental education. (To account for within-quartile variation in test scores, 1992 math and reading test scores are also included in each specification.) Differences in college enrollment by family income are particularly large for those in lower test score quartiles, both in absolute value and relative to the mean college enrollment rates in those quartiles. Among those with 1992 math test scores in the bottom quarter of the class, the gap in postsecondary school entry rates with those in the top and bottom income quintiles was 27 percentage points without conditioning on parental education and 18 points with parental education included. Both differences are large relative to the mean postsecondary entry rate of 52.2 percent.

However, table 4-3 shows fairly large differences in college entry by family income even among those with test scores in the top quartile of the class. For the students with math test scores in the top 25 percent of the class in 1992, the gap in college enrollment was a statistically significant 12 and 14 percentage points, with and without controls for parental education, respectively.

Differences among Those with Similar Class Ranks at the Same High Schools

To the extent that test scores are inadequate measures of differences in educational preparation, one may still overstate the relationship between family income and college entry. Table 4-4 reflects another strategy for identifying differences in college entry by family income that incorporates measures of high school performance. The National Education Longitudinal Study of 1988 began with a stratified sample of high schools and of students within the same schools. As a result, many in the sample attended the same schools. As part of the 1992 follow-up the high schools were asked to report school transcript information, including class rank. (Rank was available on the transcripts of 74 percent of the sample of high school graduates.) Using these data, the specifications in table 4-4 include a different fixed effect for each quintile of high school class rank within each high school. Doing so accounts both for the fact that students attending different high schools may have different academic preparation to attend college and for the fact that those in the top fifth of one high school may be less likely to attend college than those in the bottom fifth of another. Therefore table 4-4 reports differences in college entry by family income among those with similar ranks at the same high schools.

The first column shows the family income differentials in college entry pooling the sample of youth from various quintiles within high schools. (Test scores from 1992 and percentile class rank are also included as additional regressors.) The differences are still large. The gap in college entry between youth with similar high school ranks at the same high schools from the top and bottom quintiles of family income was 14 and 18 percentage points, with and without indicators for parental education included. The remaining columns of table 4-4 estimate the differences separately for those in the top and bottom half of their high school class. The differences by family income were large and statistically significant for both, with or without indicators of parental education included. However, the magnitude of the gaps again appeared to be larger for those in the bottom of their high school class.

The Sensitivity of College Enrollment to Tuition Increases

Even though there are large differences in college enrollment among those with different family incomes, the evidence does not necessarily imply that financial constraints prevent college enrollment. There could be other reasons—peer pressure, lack of familiarity with college choices, and so on. To learn more about the potential role of financing difficulties in producing such differences, one must learn something about the relationship between college cost and enrollment rates and the gap in college enrollment rates between high- and low-income youth.

When combined with differences in enrollment rates by state, state differences in tuition policies provide one way to test the importance of financing difficulties. Even though young people around the country face the same federal financial aid rules, there are large differences among states in the tuition charged at public institutions. For instance, when the National Education Longitudinal Study sample was graduating from high school in 1992, the public two-year college tuition and fees for state residents varied from $367 a year in California to $2,198 in Massachusetts. The in-state tuition for comprehensive four-year colleges ranged from $1,267 in North Carolina to $3,526 in Vermont. This

Table 4-3. *Eighth Grade Cohort of 1988 Differences in Probability of Postsecondary Enrollment by 1994, by Math Test Score Quartile in 1992*[a]

Characteristic	Bottom quartile		3d quartile		2d quartile		Top quartile	
Black, non-Hispanic	.166	.154	.114	.098	.049	.037	.089	.087
	(.030)	(.030)	(.031)	(.030)	(.033)	(.033)	(.012)	(.012)
Hispanic	.182	.182	.106	.104	.062	.058	-.016	-.013
	(.030)	(.032)	(.027)	(.029)	(.024)	(.026)	(.030)	(.030)
Other, non-Hispanic	.169	.127	.145	.121	.034	.020	.005	.003
	(.060)	(.059)	(.039)	(.039)	(.030)	(.031)	(.014)	(.014)
Family income quintile								
4th	.067	.049	.068	.053	.064	.058	.097	.087
	(.032)	(.032)	(.033)	(.033)	(.036)	(.036)	(.038)	(.038)
3d	.107	.074	.117	.094	.109	.095	.083	.070
	(.033)	(.034)	(.032)	(.033)	(.035)	(.035)	(.036)	(.036)
2d	.196	.139	.157	.108	.149	.121	.111	.095
	(.036)	(.037)	(.033)	(.034)	(.034)	(.034)	(.035)	(.035)
Top	.271	.183	.281	.192	.200	.139	.143	.118
	(.040)	(.042)	(.032)	(.035)	(.032)	(.033)	(.034)	(.034)
p-value on H_0: family income = 0	.000	.000	.000	.000	.000	.000	.000	.000
Mean postsecondary entry	.522		.719		.844		.936	
Parental education dummies included	No	Yes	No	Yes	No	Yes	No	Yes

Source: Author's calculations based on the National Education Longitudinal Study of 1988.
a. Estimated with a linear probability model. Huber-White standard errors in parentheses allow for arbitrary correlation across individuals attending the same high schools. Standardized reading and math test scores in 1992 were also included in each specification.

Table 4-4. *Eighth Grade Cohort of 1988 Differences in Probability of Postsecondary Enrollment by 1994, by High School and Class Rank Quartile in 1992*[a]

Characteristic	With high school*class rank quintile fixed effects					
	Total		Bottom half		Top half	
Black,	.089	.078	.165	.145	.042	.038
non-Hispanic	(.043)	(.044)	(.098)	(.096)	(.046)	(.046)
Hispanic	.068	.073	.138	.138	.007	.011
	(.040)	(.040)	(.087)	(.089)	(.044)	(.044)
Other,	.026	.014	.066	.044	.002	−.005
non-Hispanic	(.034)	(.034)	(.098)	(.096)	(.033)	(.033)
Family income quintile						
4th	.082	.065	.093	.064	.066	.056
	(.035)	(.035)	(.070)	(.072)	(.042)	(.042)
3d	.107	.087	.129	.101	.082	.069
	(.034)	(.034)	(.070)	(.071)	(.040)	(.040)
2d	.158	.127	.201	.152	.122	.103
	(.033)	(.034)	(.068)	(.070)	(.038)	(.039)
Top	.182	.136	.230	.171	.146	.117
	(.034)	(.035)	(.073)	(.079)	(.040)	(.042)
p-value on H_0: family income = 0	.000	.001	.013	.193	.001	.037
Mean post-secondary entry	.775		.624		.880	
Parent education dummies included	No	Yes	No	Yes	No	Yes

Source: Author's calculations based on the National Education Longitudinal Study of 1988.

a. Huber-White standard errors in parentheses allow for arbitrary correlation across individuals attending the same high schools. They were estimated using a linear probability model. Also included were the reading and math test scores in 1992 and high school class rank. The sample size of 6,678 was smaller than in previous tables due to missing values on the high school class rank variable.

section presents differences in enrollment in high- and low-tuition states to learn about the importance of tuition policies in affecting the enrollment decisions of different groups of youth.

Using the NELS sample, table 4-5 shows the relationship between postsecondary enrollment rates and state tuition and state financial aid policies.[13] With three-quarters of those entering postsecondary

13. The linear probability specifications include state unemployment rates as well. For similar results using the October Current Population Survey see Kane (1994). For additional results using the National Longitudinal Survey of Youth and the High School and Beyond survey, see Kane (1995).

Table 4-5. *Differences in Postsecondary Enrollment by State Tuition and Financial Aid Policy and Family Income Quintile*[a]

| | | Separated by family income | | | Pooled Interaction with top 60 percent in pooled |
| | | | | | |
Item	Pooled	Bottom 40 percent	Top 60 percent	Difference	sample
	Including two-year and four-year tuition				
Public two-year tuition	−.045	−.032	−.057	−.025	.006
($1,000)	(.017)	(.037)	(.019)	(.041)	(.036)
Public four-year tuition	−.008	−.052	.016	.068	.044
($1,000)	(.013)	(.029)	(.009)	(.030)	(.025)
State unemployment rate	.008	.030	−.005	−.035	−.036
	(.004)	(.008)	(.004)	(.009)	(.008)
State need-based grant spending	.242	.073	.328	.255	−.234
($1,000/person aged 15–24)	(.091)	(.238)	(.122)	(.267)	(.248)
p-value on H_0: tuition two-year, tuition four-year = 0	.000	.003	.015	. . .	.014
	Including only two-year tuition				
Public two-year tuition	−.052	−.072	−.044	.028	.052
($1,000)	(.013)	(.028)	(.018)	(.033)	(.025)
State unemployment rate	.007	.024	−.003	−.027	−.031
	(.003)	(.007)	(.004)	(.008)	(.007)
State need-based grant spending	.249	.104	.311	.207	−.171
($1,000/person aged 15–24)	(.089)	(.262)	(.123)	(.289)	(.246)
State dummies	No	No	No	. . .	Yes
Mean entry rate	.775	.614	.824	. . .	.775
N	8,164	2,830	5,334	. . .	8,164

Sources: Davis, Nastelli, and Redd (1994). Data for 1993 on spending on need-based grants by state are from the National Association of State Scholarship and Grant Programs and were merged with the NELS data (after dividing by the number of 15- to 24-year-olds in the state reported by the Bureau of the Census). Tuition data were obtained from the State of Washington's Higher Education Coordinating Board.

a. Estimated using a linear probability model. Huber-White standard errors in parentheses allow for arbitrary correlation across individuals attending high schools in the same state. Also included were the reading and math test scores in 1992, dummies for family income quintile, parental education category, and race-ethnicity and region.

education going to public institutions, for those uncertain about entering college, the average tuition for in-state students at public two-year or four-year colleges is likely to be the relevant price. In these estimates, I assume that the supply in the public sector is completely responsive to demand. Because more than 90 percent of those applying to state institutions that are not selective report being accepted at their first-choice schools, this seems a reasonable simplification. This is only fortuitous, though, because it would be difficult to construct any other structure, given the statistical difficulties of estimating the determinants of the demand for college and the supply of college slots separately. Data for 1993 on spending on need-based grants by state were acquired from the National Association of State Scholarship and Grant Programs and were merged with the NELS data (after dividing by the number of 15- to 24-year-olds in the state as reported by the Bureau of the Census).[14]

The first column of table 4-5 reports the results from pooling the NELS sample, estimating the relationship between postsecondary enrollment decisions and the combination of individual characteristics and state characteristics already described.[15] A $1,000 difference in public two-year and four-year tuition was associated with 4.5 and 0.8 percentage point declines in college enrollment, respectively. This would be consistent with the hypothesis that it is public two-year tuition that is most relevant for those who might not attend college at all. Cecilia Rouse has also reported that two-year college tuition is the relevant price for those on the margin. In addition, a 1 percentage point difference in unemployment rates across states was associated with a 0.8 percentage point increase in postsecondary enrollment. In states with higher rates of unemployment, and presumably lower opportunity costs for college students, postsecondary enrollment rates seem higher.[16]

The second and third columns of table 4-5 estimate the relationship separately for those in the bottom 40 percent of the parental income distribution and those in the top 60 percent. I will focus on the estimates excluding public four-year college tuition. (Public two-year and four-year tuition is highly correlated by state, making it difficult to identify

14. Davis, Nastelli, and Redd (1994).

15. The Huber-White standard errors were calculated allowing for arbitrary correlations across individuals attending high schools in the same state.

16. Rouse (1994). State spending on need-based grants was also positively associated with postsecondary enrollment, but this finding was much less robust.

the distinct effect of each.) A $1,000 difference in state public two-year tuition amounts is associated with a 7.2 percentage point decline in enrollment for low-income youth and a 4.4 percentage point decline for high-income youth. Differences in postsecondary entry associated with state differences in unemployment rates also seem larger for low-income youth.

The last column of table 4-5 pools the sample of high- and low-income youth, including a full set of state fixed effects. Although it is no longer possible to identify the effect of tuition policies on the enrollment rates while including state fixed effects, it is possible to identify the relationship between state tuition policies and the *gaps* in college entry by family income. The positive coefficient on the interaction between tuition and the indicator for high-income youth suggests that higher tuition levels are associated with wider gaps in enrollment rates between high- and low-income youth. There is also evidence that higher state unemployment rates are associated with smaller gaps in college enrollment by family income, possibly reflecting the greater sensitivity of low-income people to opportunity costs.

Finally, the interaction between family income and need-based grant spending was not statistically different from zero. This was puzzling because one might have expected state need-based grant spending to be associated primarily with enrollment of lower-income students, if at all. For this reason, one should treat the results for state grant spending with caution.

Effects of Within-State Changes in Tuition and the Business Cycle

Although similar estimates form the basis of conventional wisdom on the effects of tuition on going to college, an important weakness is that they are primarily identified by rather permanent differences between the states in the levels of tuition charged. Figure 4-2 shows public four-year college tuition levels in 1972, 1982, and 1992. If states had not changed tuition levels at all, the points would lie along the 45° lines. If they had raised their tuition levels by the same amount, all of the points would lie along a line parallel to the 45° lines. The figure suggests that low-tuition states have for the most part always been low-tuition states and the same has been true for high-tuition states. And when they raise tuition they tend to do so in unison. As a matter for

Figure 4-2. *Changes in Public Four-Year College Annual Tuition, by State,*
1972, 1982, 1992

Tuition in 1982 (1991 dollars)

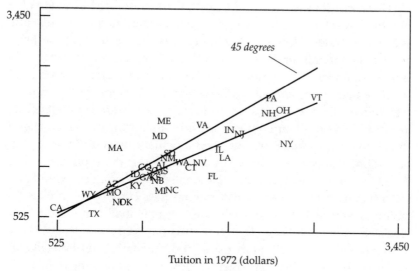

Tuition in 1972 (dollars)

Tuition in 1992 (1991 dollars)

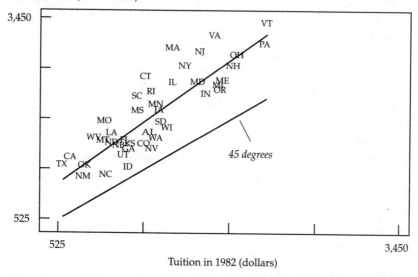

Tuition in 1982 (dollars)

Source: Tuition data collected by the State of Washington's Higher Education Coordinating Board.

statistical inference, then, it is difficult to distinguish the impact of tuition from any other characteristic of a state that would have remained constant over time.

That some states raised tuition more than others can be used to identify the importance of financing issues in accounting for differences in enrollment rates. However, the states that raised their tuition levels were not a random draw with respect to other factors that might influence enrollment rates. Figure 4-3 shows trends in average tuition levels and average unemployment rates by region, after removing region and year effects from both series.[17] Tuition increases are countercyclical, occurring when unemployment is high: the northeast, which experienced the greatest increases in unemployment rates during the latest recession, also saw the largest tuition increases; the southeast, which fared well in the last recession, saw smaller increases. This would pose no difficulty if one believed that the business cycle were unrelated to going to college. But forgone earnings are potentially important in the decision to enter college. Therefore, it is necessary to distinguish between the effects of tuition increases and economic conditions in various ways by including state unemployment rates and time trends.

Few household surveys have a sufficient sample of youth within states to evaluate changes in enrollment rates in response to changes in tuition within states. To generate accurate estimates of these changes, I pooled administrative data on fall undergraduate enrollments for more than 3,000 postsecondary institutions from 1980 through 1992.[18] In collecting this information, the U.S. Department of Education conducts a census of all postsecondary institutions in the country; therefore, the data should provide a fairly accurate measure of the changes. Total fall undergraduate enrollment (full time and part time) was summed by state and year at public and private two-year and four-year colleges. (Data from private, for-profit institutions granting less than a two-year degree were not used because of changes in the Department of

17. Each series is simply the residual from a regression equation including census division and year-specific dummies.

18. These data were obtained from the Integrated Postsecondary Education Data System data on opening fall enrollments as provided by the Computer Aided Science Policy Analysis and Research (CASPAR) Database System. The CASPAR data were developed for the National Science Foundation and are available from the Quantum Research Corporation, 7315 Wisconsin Avenue, Bethesda, MD 20814.

Figure 4-3. *Off-Trend Unemployment Rates and Tuition, by Region, 1976–92*

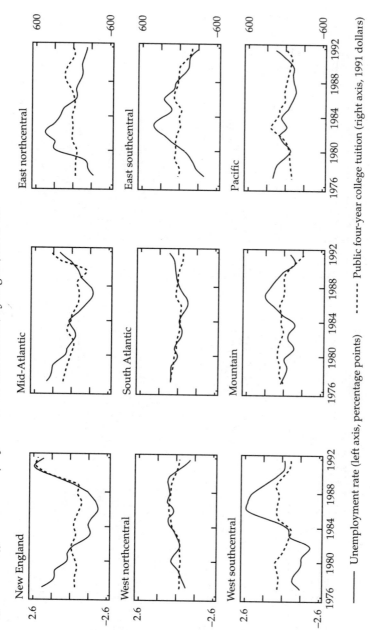

—— Unemployment rate (left axis, percentage points)   ------ Public four-year college tuition (right axis, 1991 dollars)

Source: Author's analysis of adult unemployment data from the Bureau of Labor Statistics and tuition data collected by the State of Washington's Higher Education Coordinating Board.

Table 4-6. *Relationships between Within-State Variation in Public College Enrollment and Changes in Tuition and the Business Cycle*[a]

	ln(undergraduate enrollment)			ln(white enrollment)			ln(black enrollment)		
Variable	Total public	Public two-year	Public four-year	Total public	Public two-year	Public four-year	Total public	Public two-year	Public four-year
Public two-year tuition increases ($1,000)	-.121 (.045)	-.149 (.092)	-.039 (.027)	-.050 (.074)	-.097 (.142)	.064 (.063)	.086 (.135)	-.048 (.224)	.144 (.112)
Public four-year tuition increases ($1,000)	-.073 (.029)	-.025 (.052)	-.096 (.020)	-.105 (.052)	-.055 (.093)	-.137 (.042)	-.167 (.103)	-.067 (.146)	-.214 (.087)
Unemployment rate (x.xx)	.011 (.002)	.021 (.005)	.003 (.002)	.006 (.003)	.010 (.007)	.001 (.003)	.024 (.006)	.026 (.009)	.022 (.005)
State need-based grant spending ($1,000/person aged 15–24)	.552 (.256)	.967 (.401)	.415 (.245)	.054 (.583)	.218 (.719)	.025 (.778)	2.234 (1.886)	4.153 (2.482)	.263 (1.687)
Other variables	Year dummies			Year dummies			Year dummies		
State fixed effects	Yes			Yes			Yes		
N	546			287			287		
	(42 states × 13 years)			(41 states × 7 years)			(41 states × 7 years)		

Source: Author's tabulations of panel data set of enrollment at public two- and four-year colleges by state and year, 1979 through 1991, based on Integrated Postsecondary Education Data System data on opening fall enrollments, as provided by the Computer Aided Science Policy Analysis and Research (CASPAR) Database System. The CASPAR data were developed for the National Science Foundation and are available from the Quantum Research Corporation, 7315 Wisconsin Avenue, Bethesda, Md. 20814.

a. See text for specification used. Any state with missing data on tuition or enrollment for any year was dropped from the full analysis. Regression was weighted by square root of the population of 18- to 24-year-olds in 1990 census. Data by race available only in 1980, 1982, 1984, 1986, 1988, 1990, 1991.

Education's sampling frame in the late 1980s.) To be consistent with earlier results, the same measures of tuition at public two-year and four-year colleges were used by state and year.

Table 4-6 shows the results of specifications of the following form:

$$r_{jt} = Z_{jt}\gamma + \delta_j + \theta_t + \epsilon_{jt},$$

where r_{jt} is the log of enrollment in state j in year t; Z_{jt} is a vector of time-varying state characteristics including tuition levels, the unemployment rate, and spending per capita on need-based grants within the states; δ_j represents state fixed effects; and θ_t represents year effects. Because state effects and individual year effects are included, the results in table 4-6 show the relationship between within-state changes in the log of college enrollment and changes in tuition at public two-year and four-year colleges in the state.

The results suggest large effects of within-state changes in tuition policies and the business cycle on enrollment in public colleges. (Because the dependent variable is defined in terms of log enrollment, the coefficients can be interpreted as approximating percentage changes.) A $1,000 annual increase in a state's public two-year college tuition was associated with a 12 percent decline in undergraduate enrollment. A similar rise in public four-year college tuition was associated with a 7 percent decline in enrollment. A 1 percentage point rise in unemployment is associated with a 1 percent increase in enrollment. Within-state changes in state need-based grant spending are also positively associated with aggregate enrollment in column 1, but as in table 4-5, the result is particularly unstable in other specifications.

Enrollment in public two-year colleges is especially responsive to changes in two-year college tuition levels, falling by 14.9 percent for every $1,000 increase (column 2). Public two-year college enrollment is not associated with four-year college tuition levels. However, public four-year college enrollment is very sensitive to public four-year college tuition, falling by nearly 10 percent for every $1,000 increase. The estimated relationship between public two-year college tuition and public four-year college enrollment is not statistically distinguishable from zero.

Community colleges and four-year colleges seem to face very different patterns of enrollment over the business cycle. A 1 point increase in the aggregate unemployment rate is associated with a 2.1 percentage point rise in enrollment at community colleges. The same increase in unemployment has no statistically identifiable effect on public four-year college enrollment.

Table 4-6 also shows similar results by race. Given the smaller number of years for which racial enrollment data are available, the estimates are generally less precise. However, two results stand out. First, both blacks and whites attending two-year and four-year institutions seem to be very sensitive to variations in tuition. A $1,000 increase in public four-year college tuition is associated with an 11 percent decline in white enrollment and a 17 percent decline in black enrollment. Second, although community college enrollment by whites seems to vary across the business cycle, rising by 1 percent for every 1 percentage point increase in unemployment, black enrollment at both two-year and four-year colleges seems to be particularly sensitive to business cycle changes. A 1 percentage point rise in the adult unemployment rate is associated with a 2.6 percent increase in community college enrollment and a 2.2 percent rise in public four-year college enrollment.

Figure 4-4 shows trends in college tuition and enrollment rates in Massachusetts and the other New England states (Maine, New Hampshire, Vermont, Connecticut, and Rhode Island) between 1980 and 1992. New England provides a powerful test of the effects of within-state changes in tuition, given the size of the tuition increases in Massachusetts in the late 1980s. To adjust for any preexisting differences between Massachusetts and the other New England states, the figure shows the difference in each of these measures relative to their difference in 1980. The panel on the left shows changes in the difference in public two-year and four-year college tuition as well as in need-based grant spending, while the panel on the right reports differences in enrollment ratios.[19] Changes in the difference in unemployment rates were small, given that the data were from New England only. The differentials in enrollment followed each of the changes in the differential in costs. The gap in enrollment between Massachusetts and the remainder of New England widened at the beginning of the 1980s when tuition differences grew. The Massachusetts advantage then began to increase when need-based grant spending rose relative to that of other

---

19. To be more comparable to the tuition data, need-based grant spending per person aged 15–24 is multiplied by 5 because the ratio of enrollment to the population aged 15–24 is roughly 0.2.

Figure 4-4. *Differences in College Costs and Enrollment Ratios,
Massachusetts versus Other New England States
(Differences in Differences), 1980–92*

Dollars

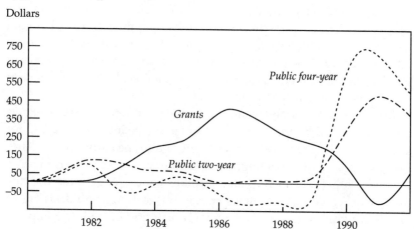

Percent difference in enrollment

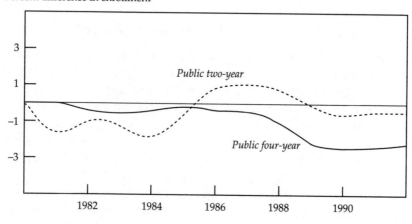

Source: See table 4-6.

states in the mid-1980s, particularly at two-year colleges. In the late
1980s and early 1990s, when Massachusetts raised tuitions more than
the other states and cut grant spending, Massachusetts's advantage
then decreased. As reflected in the regression results in table 4-6, within-
state increases in tuition do seem to be reflected in enrollment declines.

It is worth noting that governors and state legislators are likely to have been misled during the 1980s and early 1990s if they used their own states' experience to infer the sensitivity of college enrollment to increases in tuition. Figure 1-1 showed that college enrollment rates rose between 1980 and 1995, presumably reflecting the effect of changing labor market conditions. So even as a state raised its tuition, it was likely to see enrollments continue to increase. It is only the difference in enrollment trends relative to other states that reveals the importance of tuition hikes on college enrollment rates.

In a 1999 study Susan Dynarski exploited a different "natural experiment" provided by the termination of special college financial aid for survivors under the social security program in the early 1980s.[20] After the tuition benefit was eliminated, enrollment rates of those with a deceased father declined relative to other youth—suggesting that the loss of the benefit had an impact on the college enrollment decisions of youth in families receiving survivor's benefits. Indeed, the implied enrollment response per dollar increase in the net cost of college was very similar to the estimates already summarized.

How Sensitive Are Youth to the Cost of College?

The estimates of enrollment responses to tuition changes that I have presented are similar to past estimates. In their review of twenty-five estimates of tuition price responses as of 1988, Larry Leslie and Paul Brinkman found that the median estimate suggested a $1,000 increase in annual tuition costs is associated with a 5 percentage point decrease in postsecondary entry, which is similar to the results shown in table 4-5.[21] Using data from the National Longitudinal Survey of Youth, Stephen Cameron and James Heckman have estimated that a $1,000 difference in tuition is associated with a 6 percentage point difference in enrollment.[22] Michael McPherson and Morton Schapiro and Thomas J. Kane report similar estimates.[23] The relationship between community college enroll-

---

20. Dynarski (1999).

21. Leslie and Brinkman (1988). Their estimate was that a $100 increase in tuition in 1982–83 dollars was associated with a 0.7 percentage point decline in enrollment among 18- to 24-year-olds. See their appendix table 6.

22. Cameron and Heckman (1998).

23. McPherson and Schapiro (1991a); Kane (1994); and Kane (1995).

ment and the business cycle shown in table 4-6 is similar to that reported by Julian Betts and Laurel McFarland, albeit slightly smaller.[24]

Yet particularly when considering the fact that tuition represents only a small share of the cost of a year of higher education, all these estimates imply strikingly large elasticities of demand. For instance, in 1992 the average annual tuition for an in-state student at a public two-year institution was $1,025, and the average income of a male 18- to 24-year-old high school graduate working full time year round was $16,916.[25] If a full-time student forfeited nine out of twelve months of the average earnings of a high school graduate, the total cost of a year in college would have been $13,712 ($1,025 in tuition and $12,687 in forgone salary). A $1,000 increase in tuition would represent a 7.3 percent increase in cost. Combining these figures with the results from table 4-5, one finds that a 7.3 percent increase in cost is associated with a 6.7 percent (0.052/0.775) decline in enrollment, implying an elasticity of about –1.

One can also calculate the price elasticity with respect to opportunity costs, using the evidence on the relationship between enrollment and the business cycle. If u_y represents an unemployment rate for teenagers and w the earnings of employed high school graduates, the expected earnings of a young high school graduate could be expressed as $(1 - u_y)w$. The change in the expected wage with respect to a change in the overall unemployment rate is simply $-w$ times the change in youth unemployment rate per unit change in the overall unemployment rate. (A time series regression of the annual average unemployment rate for 16- to 19-year-olds on the civilian unemployment rate from 1972 to 1996 implies that youth unemployment rises by 1.62 points for every 1 point increase in total unemployment.) Using these figures and the mean earnings of 18- to 24-year-old high school graduates, a 1 point increase in unemployment would lead to an estimated $206 decrease in expected earnings (0.0162 $\times$ [–16,916] $\times$ [9 months/12 months]). Five times the coefficient on the unemployment rate in column 1 of table 4-5 is 3.5, implying that a $1,000 difference in opportunity costs related to business cycle changes is associated with a 3.5 percent decline in enrollment. This is only slightly smaller than the 6.7 percent decline associated with a $1,000 rise in tuition. Therefore, the estimated elasticities with respect to tuition and unemployment are both quite consistent and quite large.

24. Betts and McFarland (1995).
25. National Center for Education Statistics (1997b, table 312).

Are Youth More Sensitive to College Costs Than to Labor Market Payoffs?

How do these elasticities compare with the enrollment response to the 1980s' widening wage differentials based on educational attainment? As is well known, the gaps in annual earnings by educational attainment widened dramatically between 1980 and 1992 for all age groups (table 4-7). The annual earnings gap for men 25 to 34 years old between those with some college and those with only a high school degree grew by 210 percent. The gap for those aged 35–44 and 45–54 grew by 73 percent and 96 percent, respectively. Using various discount rates, I estimated the present value of such earnings differentials for people aged 21, assuming that future earnings differentials mirror the earnings differentials in the cross-section in 1980 and 1992. Using a 6 percent discount rate, the estimated present value of future earnings differentials associated with attending some college increased by 116 percent between 1980 and 1992 from $37,400 to $80,664. The estimated value associated with completing a college degree grew from $144,077 to $226,132, a 57 percent increase.

The proportion of high school graduates entering college increased as the payoff to schooling increased. Yet postsecondary enrollment rates increased only from 65 to 72 percent (table 4-7).[26] This 7 percentage point rise in college entry represented an 11 percent rise in enrollment (0.07/0.65), implying an elasticity of only 0.10, using the growth in the present value of the differential between high school graduates and those with some college, and 0.21, using the differential between high school graduates and college graduates. This difference between the response to the cost of college, with large elasticities with respect to tuition variation and wide countercyclical swings in enrollment, and the comparatively muted response to the rise in the labor market value of a college education would be consistent with behavior in the presence of financing constraints. If there is a high marginal cost of capital, students and families respond sharply to changes in the cost of college but respond more sluggishly to increases in the payoff.

---

26. This figure is different from the one-third increase in enrollment rates of 18- to 24-year-olds mentioned in chapter 1. However, because all the tuition and unemployment estimates refer to the difference in college entry rates, as opposed to the stock of college students, this latter comparison is more appropriate.

Table 4-7. *Full-Time, Full-Year Earnings of Men, by Age and Educational Attainment, 1980 and 1992*

Constant 1992 dollars unless otherwise specified

Age and educational attainment	1980	1992	Percent change
Aged 25–34			
High school graduates	28,817	24,403	–15
Some college	30,466	29,508	–3
Four or more years of college	36,412	39,972	10
Differentials			
Some college – high school graduate	1,649	5,105	210
Four or more years of college –			
high school graduate	7,595	15,569	105
Aged 35–44			
High school graduates	33,958	30,226	–11
Some college	38,747	38,523	–1
Four or more years of college	51,563	56,274	9
Differentials			
Some college – high school graduate	4,790	8,297	73
Four or more years of college –			
high school graduate	17,605	26,048	48
Aged 45–54			
High school graduates	35,204	33,182	–6
Some college	41,919	46,324	11
Four or more years of college	58,576	61,002	4
Differentials			
Some college – high school graduate	6,715	13,142	96
Four or more years of college –			
high school graduate	23,373	27,820	19
Percent of recent high school graduates			
entering postsecondary within two years	64.6	72.3	12

Source: Author's calculations based on Bureau of the Census (1995, Historical Income Tables P27, P28A).

Evaluating the Pell Grant Program

The evidence I have presented suggests that low-income young people are less likely to attend college, even after controlling for academic preparation, and that the gaps in enrollment by family income are particularly wide in the states with high tuitions. How effective has federal financial aid policy been in closing these gaps?

In 1973 the Pell Grant program was established to provide grant aid to low-income youth. Because the program affected only low-income people, one might have expected their enrollment rates to have increased disproportionately compared with those of wealthier peers.[27] In an article that prompted a firestorm of criticism, W. Lee Hansen reported little growth in enrollment of low-income young people during the 1970s.[28] McPherson and Schapiro identified two weaknesses in Hansen's methodology. He used only two years of data on either side of the policy change, presumably weakening the power of his test.[29] And by pooling men and women, the program effect he estimated was contaminated by any change in college-going behavior by men at the end of the Vietnam War.

To address both of these concerns, table 4-8 shows the program effect for women only and pools eight years of data. The data from the October Current Population Survey are broken into two periods: 1970–72 (before the program was established) and 1973–77. The growth in enrollment rates for those from families in the lowest-income quartile (most of whom would have been eligible for Pell Grants) is then compared with the trend in enrollment rates for those from the top three quartiles. Three different dependent variables are used: total college enrollment rates, enrollment rates in private universities, and enrollment rates in public two-year institutions. Total college enrollment rates grew 2.6 percentage points more *slowly* for the lowest-income quartile over the period (although this difference was not significantly different from zero). Private college enrollment grew 2.8 percentage points *less* for low-income youth over the period. Only public two-year college enrollment seemed to grow more quickly for low-income youth. (However, one must bear in mind that total college enrollment rates did not increase more rapidly, suggesting that there may have been some relative shifts in enrollment among different types of colleges.) As shown in columns 2, 4, and 6, adding family background measures such as parental education and home ownership has little effect on the results.[30]

---

27. Amendments in 1978 would open the program to middle-class students. For a description see Manski and Wise (1983).

28. Hansen (1983).

29. McPherson and Schapiro (1991b).

30. Not all time series evidence yields similarly small estimates of the effect of cost on enrollment. For instance, McPherson and Schapiro (1991a) use national aggregate time series data on enrollment rates of low-income white students, finding that the rates declined by 6 points for every $1,000 increase in net direct costs. Although the estimate is

Table 4-8. *Changes in College Enrollment Rates of Dependent 18- to 19-Year-Old Women, by Family-Income Quartile, 1970–72 to 1973–77*[a]

Independent variable	Any college enrollment		Private college enrollment		Public two-year college enrollment	
Black	−.027	.044	.000	.034	−.029	.000
	(.023)	(.020)	(.013)	(.013)	(.014)	(.013)
Postwar (1973–77)	.025	−.008	.022	−.003	−.009	−.010
	(.010)	(.010)	(.006)	(.005)	(.007)	(.007)
Black*postwar	.027	−.015	−.010	−.027	.005	.012
	(.028)	(.025)	(.016)	(.015)	(.018)	(.017)
Lowest-income	−.026	.005	−.028	−.002	.034	.024
quartile*postwar	(.023)	(.022)	(.013)	(.009)	(.015)	(.015)
Family background included	No	Yes	No	Yes	No	Yes
N	12,163	12,163	12,163	12,163	12,163	12,163

Source: Author's calculations based on October Current Population Survey data for 1970–72 and 1973–76.

a. Estimated within a linear probability framework. Included in all equations were dummy variables for income quartiles, region, and a constant term. Family background measures included ten dummy variables for the education of parents and home ownership.

This evidence certainly presents a challenge to the current financial aid system. It is not simply that one would have expected the effect of Pell Grants to have been small: the maximum grant in 1975 would have been $4,200 in 1998 dollars. On the basis of the cross-section estimates, one would have expected low-income youth receiving the maximum grant to have increased enrollment rates by more than 20 percentage points.

The Job Training Partnership Act Evaluation

One hypothesis to reconcile Hansen's findings with the other results in this chapter is that low-income families' lack of information

---

similar to the ones reported in cross-sectional work, it is based primarily on the common timing of a decline in enrollment rates for low-income youth in the early 1980s and an increase in state tuition levels. But many other things were changing during these years. For instance, both trends coincided with a serious recession. With only time variation in costs and enrollment rates, it is impossible to distinguish the effect of tuition increases from other unmeasured changes that may have occurred and affected the national market for a college education.

about financial aid programs blunts their impact. Students can read about tuition hikes in the local newspapers, but they may invest the time to learn about the availability of financial aid only if they are fairly committed to attending college. A number of surveys have shown parents to be confused about financial aid programs.[31] But it is difficult to sort out cause from effect since those people most committed to going to college would be more likely to have or to seek the information.

The ideal policy experiment would be to lower the barriers to applying for aid for a random group of young people and observe any differences in college enrollment relative to a control group. Essentially, this was the experiment performed by the Job Training Partnership Act evaluation. In monetary terms the JTPA program did not offer treatment group members much that they did not already qualify for. (Tables 4-9 and 4-10 contain data from James Heckman and colleagues on the private costs and enrollment rates of those assigned to the classroom training subgroup of the JTPA experiment.[32]) For adult women entering training, the average private cost of a month of classroom instruction was $100 for the control group, $76 more than the cost for those in the treatment group. But during the eighteen months following random assignment, 56 percent of the women in the treatment group received some classroom training compared with 34 percent of those in the control group, implying a 22 percentage point impact on entry rates into classroom training. The enrollment effects were large for all the subgroups assigned to classroom training: a 22 percentage point increase for adults and young men and a 19 percentage point increase for young women. These enrollment responses imply elasticities much larger than those estimated using state differences in tuition policies. Given the modest effects of JTPA on the actual monetary costs of training, the magnitude of the enrollment effects is remarkable. One reason may be that JTPA not only lowered the monetary costs of training, but also lessened the nonmonetary costs of applying for financial aid and locating an appropriate program.

---

31. See, for example, Carroll (1983); Brouder (1987); Little and Chronister (1983); and Higgins (1984).
32. Heckman and others (forthcoming).

Table 4-9. *Adult Male and Female Entry Rates and the Costs of Classroom Training in the JTPA Experiment (Classroom Training Subgroup Only)*

Item	Treatment group	Control group	Difference (p-value)
Adult men			
Percent receiving classroom training	49	27	22 (.00)
Average total hours of training per trainee (18 months)	670	694	−24 (.76)
Percent of trainees with nonzero private expenditures	16	41	−25 (.00)
Average monthly payment per trainee (dollars)	199	340	−141 (.44)
Annual payment per trainee (dollars) (12*average monthly payment)	2,396	4,087	−1,690 (.44)
Implied enrollment response per $1,000 annual cost	. . .	. . .	−.13
Adult women			
Percent receiving classroom training	56	34	22 (.00)
Average total hours of training per trainee (18 months)	707	779	−72 (.16)
Percent of trainees with nonzero private expenditures	11	39	−28 (.00)
Average monthly payment per trainee (dollars)	24	100	−73 (.00)
Annual payment per trainee (dollars) (12*average monthly payment)	293	1,198	−905 (.00)
Implied enrollment response per $1,000 annual cost	. . .	. . .	−.24

Source: Heckman and others (forthcoming).

Extraordinary Returns to Schooling

One further test of financing constraints for low-income young people would be to look for differences in the incremental payoffs to schooling for those from high- and low-income families. If low-income people are financially constrained, one might expect to see higher rates of return for them on the margin than for youth with more ready access to capital. The difficulty comes in trying to estimate the return to schooling for

Table 4-10. *Male and Female Youth Entry Rates and the Costs of Classroom Training in the JTPA Experiment (Classroom Training Subgroup Only)*

Item	Treatment group	Control group	Difference (p-value)
Male youth			
Percent receiving classroom training	56	34	22 (.00)
Average total hours of training per trainee (18 months)	744	696	48 (.66)
Percent of trainees with nonzero private expenditures	16	48	−32 (.00)
Average monthly payment per trainee (dollars)	37	102	−65 (.01)
Annual payment per trainee (dollars) (12*averge monthly payment)	449	1,226	−777 (.01)
Implied enrollment response per $1,000 annual cost	. . .	. . .	−.28
Female youth			
Percent receiving classroom training	59	40	19 (.00)
Average total hours of training per trainee (18 months)	768	591	177 (.00)
Percent of trainees with nonzero private expenditures	13	37	−24 (.00)
Average monthly payment per trainee (dollars)	45	231	−186 (.19)
Annual payment per trainee (dollars) (12*averge monthly payment)	538	2,769	2,231 (.19)
Implied enrollment response per $1,000 annual cost	. . .	. . .	−.09

Source: Heckman and others (forthcoming).

those undecided about going to college. Labor economists have disagreed for three decades on estimates of the average return to schooling, disputing whether the research controls adequately for differences before they go on to college in the abilities of those attaining higher levels of schooling. However, in an article using distance from the closest four-year college to identify the marginal return to schooling, David Card found that the marginal returns are even higher for low-income youth than for others.[33] This would be consistent with my findings above that low-income students behave as if they lack access to capital.

Incentives Provided by Parents

So far, I have not considered how families influence their children's decisions to attend college, how families structure incentives. Instead, I have simply observed that family income is related to enrolling in college and to the apparent responsiveness of young people to differences in tuition. But how is it that higher-income parents persuade their children that college is a worthwhile investment and that they should leave behind their familiar environment and go away to school, spend late nights in the library, and risk living with absolute strangers? How is it that these parents persuade their children to use their earnings from a summer job to pay tuition bills rather than buy a new car or a new stereo or a new wardrobe?

Parents can influence the behavior of children in the years leading up to college through advice, encouragement, and dinner table lectures on the importance of education. But parents also seem to resort to unabashed bribery. Those young people who responded to the National Postsecondary Student Aid Study in 1992–93 were asked to report the amount of aid they received from their parents. They were asked to distinguish parental gifts from loans for which parents explicitly expected repayment (although this distinction may become ambiguous if parents implicitly expect reciprocal gift giving) and in-kind benefits such as free room and board at the parents' home. Table 4-11 shows parental contributions to dependent students attending college full time and also the cost to students after accounting for direct parental contributions and any educational grants. The results in the table report differences after controlling for parental education, but controlling for parental education has relatively little impact on the estimates.

The second column in the top panel shows that young people from the top quintile attending public four-year colleges received an annual average parental contribution of $4,693 more than did the low-income youth from the bottom quintile. The third column reports that the difference in parental contributions is even larger for those youth attending private four-year colleges—$8,175.

33. Card (1995).

Table 4-11. *Parental Contributions and Net College Costs for Full-Time Dependent Undergraduates, by Type of College, 1992–93*[a]

Parental income quintile	Public two-year	Public four-year	Private four-year
	Parental contribution (excluding loans and in-kind benefits)		
2d	1,147	2,024	1,047
	(1,065)	(376)	(727)
3d	1,549	2,809	2,753
	(1,193)	(359)	(710)
4th	1,717	3,221	5,272
	(1,229)	(362)	(654)
Highest	2,851	4,693	8,175
	(1,251)	(353)	(618)
	Net cost to student (tuition – grant aid – parental contribution)		
2d	–290	–1,115	50
	(1,217)	(373)	(722)
3d	–597	–1,850	–1,537
	(1,362)	(356)	(706)
4th	–451	–1,997	–2,405
	(1,403)	(359)	(651)
Highest	–1,457	–3,411	–3,903
	(1,429)	(350)	(614)
N	244	2,589	1,511

Source: Author's calculations based on data from the National Postsecondary Student Aid Study, 1992–93.

a. The figures in the table are differences in parental contributions and net costs, reported relative to those from the lowest family income quintile. All the above specifications include indicators for parents' education. They also include college fixed effects. That is, they compare costs for those attending the same institutions.

Part of this difference in parental contributions is offset by the combination of federal, state, and institutional means-tested grants, but the grant aid was not large enough to offset the differences in parental contributions. Young people from low-income families paid considerably more of the cost of attending four-year colleges than higher-income youth. A student from the highest income quintile paid $3,411 less than one from the lowest income quintile to attend a public four-year college. The difference for those attending private four-year colleges was $3,903.

Thus young people from higher-income families may attend college at higher rates simply because their parents have made the choice more obvious for them by paying a larger share of the costs of attending. Indeed, if one were to take the difference in parental contribution between the bottom and top income quintiles for those attending public four-year colleges—$3,411—and multiply by my estimate of the effect of a $1,000 difference in tuition (0.06), one would predict a 20 percentage point difference in college attendance. This is comparable to the 23.6 percentage point difference in college attendance by family income quintile (controlling for test scores) shown in table 4-2.

Thus one needs no complicated framework of family decisionmaking to explain the differences in college attendance by family income. Higher-income parents subsidize the costs of college more heavily than low-income parents. If one were to take the resulting differences in cost of attendance for high- and low-income people and multiply by the estimates of the responsiveness of youth to differences in cost, one would predict differences in college attendance similar to those observed. Even if the hopes and dreams of 18-year-olds were similar regardless of the income of their parents and even if they were all similarly averse to postponing gratification regardless of their parents' incomes, differences in college enrollment rates between high- and low-income youth could be explained simply by referring to the choices their parents are able to create for them by more heavily subsidizing college attendance.

Refocusing the Debate

The debate over the extent to which financial aid helps low-income students lacks a point of reference, a compass by which to weigh the trade-offs implicit in choosing between various policy responses. In the health care debate two statistics framed the discussion: the proportion of the population covered by a health insurance plan and the measures of cost increases. There is no analogous statistic for focusing the financial aid debate. I propose using the differences in college entry rates among young people with similar test scores in their senior year in high school as an indicator of how well our financial aid system is working. Although a quarter century has passed since the inception of the Pell Grant program, financial aid policy has failed to close the gaps in college enrollment for similarly prepared students from high- and low-income families.

Figure 4-5. *Proportion of Classes of 1982 and 1992 Entering a Four-Year College or Any Postsecondary Training, by Family Income*

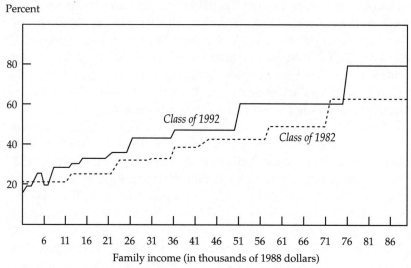

Four-year college

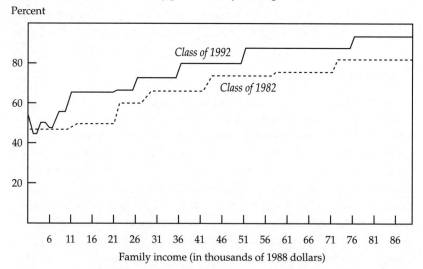

Any postsecondary training

Source: Author's tabulation of data from the High School and Beyond survey of the class of 1982 and the National Education Longitudinal Study of 1988.

As the labor market payoffs to college entry have increased, the cost of not being able to run the gauntlet of financial aid applications and finance a college education has also increased. Even if the gaps in college enrollment by family income had remained constant, the higher payoff to a college education combined with preexisting differences in college attendance by parental income would imply that parental resources have become more important than they once were in determining a young person's earning prospects, all else equal.

But the gaps in college entry by family income have not remained constant; they have widened. Figure 4-5 shows the proportion of youth entering any form of postsecondary training and the proportion entering a four-year college within two years after high school. It is clear that college enrollment rates are very different at different levels of income. It is also clear that college enrollment rates have increased. But the increases in entry into four-year colleges were larger for middle- and high-income young people than for those from low-income families.

The behavior of low-income youth would indicate that lack of ability to pay is a major impediment to investing in college. Unfortunately, the source of the problem is unclear. Even if the borrowing limits under the federal student loan programs were raised, the lack of understanding of how to apply for student financial aid may be the obstacle. An option potentially less costly than raising aid limits would be to invest more in marketing the aid programs to students, particularly those who are most likely to be unable to choose the kind of aid they need and navigate the application system.

5

Rethinking How Americans Pay for College

As labor market conditions lead more young people to attend college, the nation's financial aid system is showing signs of strain. Public school tuitions are rising, and parents are increasingly anxious about their ability to afford a college education for their children. Despite some incremental changes, the basic structure of higher education financing, with large state subsidies directed toward public institutions and means-tested federal grant and loan aid for individuals, has been in place since the mid-1970s. The purpose of this chapter is to lay the foundation for a more thoroughgoing policy debate by proposing reforms, incremental and more fundamental, to the current financial aid system. It is useful to begin by reminding ourselves of the goals of financial aid policy and to discuss some of the inevitable trade-offs to be faced in designing a financial aid system.

Goal 1: Providing Liquidity for Worthwhile Investments

As discussed in chapter 4, the first goal of financial aid policy should be to ensure that all youth have access to capital to make investments in a college education, whether or not they choose to make use of it. Even if society cared only about economic growth and not about its distribution, it would still want the government to intervene in financing such education. A college education requires an intensive use of society's resources for a relatively brief period, usually early in a person's career. The costs of faculty time as well as the student's own time outside of the labor market are considerable. Few families possess the savings to be able to finance such a large investment entirely out of their own pockets.

Private banks are unlikely to provide loans to many of those now going to college because the students lack collateral. A bank can repossess a car or foreclose on a house. But it is impossible to repossess an education or force educated people to work up to their potential so that they can repay the loan.[1]

Families serve as lending institutions for many college students. There are solid economic reasons for this tradition: parents are in a unique position to know their children's abilities and intentions regarding college and a career. Parents may know which of their children will make good use of an expensive college education and which are not ready. The need-analysis system and the calculation of an expected family contribution reinforce this tradition.

But although there may be good reasons to keep families involved, few of us live in families able to finance a $25,000-a-year loan. Therefore, societies have developed policies to help families solve this liquidity problem, diverting the necessary resources into the hands of youth at the time they most need it to attend college, whether it be operating subsidies to institutions, wage supplements for students, or grant or loan aid.

Some financing schemes are likely to be more successful than others in weeding out economically unjustifiable investments. For instance, the primary difference between a student loan and a grant is that the loan ensures that students' obligations are more closely linked to their educational choices. If students receive large institutional subsidies and pay indirectly for their education only through higher taxes later in life, there is no direct link between their schooling decisions and the amount of tax they pay. By expecting young people to pay back some share of their loan, the student loan program has a built-in guard against waste.

Loans are not the only way to encourage the young to use society's resources prudently, even in a system with large subsidies. In principle a system in which the government pays the full cost of attendance out of tax revenue could work equally well as a means of financing worthwhile

---

1. Although banks occasionally may be willing to make unsecured loans to small businesses, a small business owner is likely to be more dependent on credit in the future, so the threat of a poor credit rating is likely to be worth more to an owner than to an 18-year-old.

investments if admissions committees could successfully identify and admit only those candidates for whom a college education would pay off. Indeed, an admissions committee may often be better able than an inexperienced 18-year-old in identifying a good investment. This is the traditional European model, although, as was discussed in chapter 2, there are signs that it might be breaking down. Indeed, such a system could be expected to have difficulty adjusting when labor market conditions change, given the decrease and subsequent increase in the payoff to postsecondary training that has occurred over the past three decades. Bureaucracies may be slow to recognize when labor market conditions have changed and may find it politically difficult to restrict admission when conditions warrant it.

Goal 2: Paying for Social Benefits

A second goal of higher education finance policy is to ensure that worthwhile investments are made, even when the youth deciding about entering college is not the only one to benefit from his or her decision. We usually assume that people care primarily about their own well-being in deciding whether to enter college. To the extent that some of those who are hesitant will decide on the basis of their possible personal rewards that it is not worth the investment, the public good might be served by lowering the costs to encourage them to enroll. Ernest Pascarella and Patrick Terenzini have summarized the research suggesting that college yields other benefits such as greater tolerance for social and gender differences and a greater likelihood of participating in the electoral process.[2]

Even if social benefits are hard to measure, there can still be a fruitful discussion about the types of subsidies that are most likely to yield such benefits. Establishing the existence of social benefits is not sufficient to justify public action. One must also ask, does a subsidy actually have any effect on behavior? In fact, the magnitude of any social value created by a public subsidy for education depends equally on two dimensions: the size of the public benefit per new college entrant and the number of new entrants that are drawn into college by a given subsidy. (The former represents the "height" of the economist's "welfare triangle," while the latter represents its "width." According to the laws of

2. Pascarella and Terenzini (1991).

geometry, the area of the triangle depends equally on both.) It is probably unlikely that an extra $1,000 subsidy would have induced Microsoft chairman Bill Gates to remain in college. However, the same subsidy may induce a low-income youth to enroll in a community college to learn to be computer programmer using Gates's software.

Goal 3: Providing Insurance for College Entrants

Beyond providing the liquidity needed by those entering college and subsidizing the students who generate benefits for others, government can help provide insurance to those considering a college education. Although the average difference in earnings between a high school and college graduate grew during the 1980s, the variation in income among those with the same level of education also grew.[3] A high school graduate could reasonably expect greater earnings by attending college, but the distribution of possible outcomes for any given person has also widened. Therefore, although a college education has a higher expected payoff than before, it is also probably a riskier investment because some will have higher returns than others, and some may even face negative returns.[4] Particularly among first-generation college students, risk aversion may leave some worthwhile investments unmade.

Both grants and loans reduce risk, although to different degrees. By allowing Stafford Loan borrowers to finance college with a ten- to thirty-year term of repayment or by allowing students to qualify for forbearance during periods of unemployment, the federal government already alleviates some of the risk of borrowing. A grant obviously reduces risk as well because it need not be paid back. However, a grant is also a much more expensive way for society to reduce risk. Providing grant aid gets the insurance function backward: it is like the government paying everybody in the country $100 in case there is a flood, rather than compensating the flood victims. Easing the terms of repayment in the loan programs is an alternative way to provide such insurance.

---

3. Juhn, Murphy, and Pierce (1993).

4. This would be true as long as not all of the increase in earnings inequality was due to an increase in permanent income inequality. Moreover, even if a large share of the rise in inequality is due to an increase in permanent income inequality, those who have yet to start their labor market careers are likely to be uncertain about their own prospects, even if the prospects turn out to be relatively stable.

Goal 4: Responding to Increasing Earnings Inequality

Lowering the barriers to higher education and encouraging more youth to attend may also be advocated as a response to the deteriorating earnings prospects of the less skilled. However, as Richard Herrnstein and Charles Murray argue in *The Bell Curve*, subsidizing education, or in their example, building libraries, could simply make inequality worse if the most advantaged are more likely to take advantage of the opportunities provided.[5]

The debate is related to a decade-long dispute begun by W. Lee Hansen and Burton Weisbrod in the *Journal of Human Resources* when they concluded that public higher education in California contributed to earnings inequality.[6] They noted that the children of the wealthy were more likely to attend college than the children of the poor. Further, the children of the wealthy were more likely to attend the flagship University of California, which received much larger subsidies than the public community colleges where low-income youth often went, when they attended at all. Finally, they noted that the whole system was financed primarily by a regressive state income tax structure. Rather than ameliorating income inequality, they argued, public higher education was part of the problem.[7]

But this evidence is not sufficient to support the conclusion that higher education actually contributes to income inequality. Even with regressive state taxes, higher-income families' share of state tax revenue paid is generally larger than the share of postsecondary subsidies they receive. In other words, even though the tax rate structure in many states is regressive, high-income families still pay a large share of all tax revenues collected.[8] When Joseph Pechman and others considered taxes

5. Herrnstein and Murray (1994).

6. Hansen and Weisbrod (1969).

7. The *Journal of Human Resources* published seven responses to the article between 1970 and 1977; for instance, see Pechman (1970); Pechman (1971); Cohn (1970); Gifford (1970); Sharkansky (1970); Conlisk (1977); Hartman (1970); Hansen and Weisbrod (1971); Crean (1975); and McGuire (1976). And this does not include a number of related articles in other journals. The Hansen and Weisbrod suggestion was certainly controversial. As a number of respondents later pointed out, they had not actually calculated the net benefits of higher education by income group. Rather, their argument was based solely on two observations: that higher-income youth receive a large share of the benefits and that state taxes are often regressive.

8. Regressivity does not mean taxes paid decline with higher incomes but simply that the proportion of income paid in taxes is lower.

paid and benefits received by various income groups, they came to the conclusion that low-income youth enjoyed positive net benefits, even with regressive taxes, because the taxes paid by their families did not exceed the value of the educational benefits they received.[9]

The estimates presented in table 2-3 suggested that public spending on higher education is disproportionately enjoyed by higher income families. However, the net progressivity also depends on who is paying for these subsidies. Because it is never possible to know which taxes would be lowered if the public subsidy to higher education were eliminated, it is probably impossible to resolve the Hansen-Weisbrod-Pechman debate once and for all.[10] Pechman made the reasonable assumption that the tax rebate would be proportional to taxes paid. But even reasonable assumptions are just assumptions.

Does public higher education reduce income inequality? Probably yes, because higher-income families pay a large proportion of the state taxes used to support higher education and many low-income families receive more in subsidies than the taxes they pay. But one cannot be sure without knowing which tax revenue would be saved if subsidies were cut. Could the benefits from public subsidies be distributed more equitably? Certainly. Flagship public universities consume considerable public subsidies, and high-income youth are disproportionately represented. Further, as the price of college grew between 1980 and 1993, there is some evidence that the highest-income youth were switching from private to public universities.[11]

The Inevitable Trade-offs Limiting Public Action

In thinking about the options for designing a financing system for higher education, one must also bear in mind the trade-offs that circumscribe the options.

Trade-off 1: Means-Testing Student Aid Is a Form of Taxation

Of the nearly $50 billion in state and local subsidies to higher education, less than 10 percent is provided as state means-tested grant

9. Pechman (1970).
10. Hansen and Weisbrod (1969, p. 77).
11. McPherson and Schapiro (1998).

programs.[12] The lion's share of state and local subsidies to higher education is made in flat grants to public institutions to keep tuition low for all state residents. A number of observers, including me, have argued that more of those state resources should be means tested. The usual rationale is either an equity argument (the resources are more appropriately spent on disadvantaged youth) or an argument about program effects (targeted subsidies are more likely to affect the behavior of low-income young people and less likely simply to subsidize investments they were going to make anyway).

However, it is impossible to design a means-tested benefit formula that guarantees access of low-income youth without imposing very high tax rates on income or savings or both. In an analysis of the tax rates implied by financial aid formulas Karl Case and Michael McPherson concluded that the marginal rates are high only for those attending the most expensive private schools.[13] This is true. But it is simply a result of the fact that states also provide large subsidies that are not means tested, keeping public tuition low across the board. Where tuition is very low, most students will have parental incomes high enough that the formulas will render them ineligible for any federal aid, and as a result the marginal tax rate implied by financial aid rules is zero for many parents. In other words, higher across-the-board subsidies may mean higher state income taxes, but they also mean lower tax rates for financial aid since fewer students qualify. As a result, most students will face a zero marginal tax rate due to the financial aid formulas. As states raise public tuition, more youth will be judged to have "unmet need" and these "tax rates" will apply to a larger share of the college-going population.

One particularly dysfunctional characteristic of the financial aid formula is that these tax rates apply to a single year's income. If states were to charge the full cost of a year of education (approximately $11,000), and the federal and state governments were to provide sufficient grant funding to ensure that those with incomes of $30,000 or less faced zero net cost of tuition while those with incomes of $60,000 or more received loans instead of grants, the implicit tax rate would have to be 40 percent over the range $30,000 to $60,000. Particularly when these implicit taxes are applied on top of existing payroll and other income taxes, the aggregate tax rate would be very high for families in this range.

12. National Center for Education Statistics (1997b, table 325, p. 341).
13. Case and McPherson (1986).

Parental assets also matter in the current benefit formula. Some might defend the use of parental assets in the formulas in that they provide a more complete picture of a family's economic resources. However, basing eligibility on assets necessarily imposes a tax on savings, discouraging parents from saving for their children's education. And because the tax rates on parental assets are applied every year that one has a child enrolled in school, these rates can be high for those with children in college over a number of years. Martin Feldstein has estimated that if a family has two children who attend college consecutively for eight years, the tax rate on parental savings can be as high as 50 percent.[14]

In the formula that became effective in 1993, parental assets in a house are excluded from the calculation of eligibility. Whether or not the full implications of this exclusion were recognized by its proponents, excluding housing creates a huge loophole in the formula that may take time for parents to discover but that will essentially remove assets from consideration altogether. (Pension assets and the benefits in retirement accounts have always been excluded.) If parents simply transferred the value of all their liquid assets that exceeded the allowable limits into home equity and then took out a second mortgage to finance their child's education, they could escape the new asset test entirely. This is clearly a mixed blessing. On the one hand, the implicit tax rate on savings has been reduced. On the other hand, federal aid is much less well targeted.

To the extent that tax-savvy parents find ways to shift assets into home equity, the remaining asset test has become a tax on nonstrategic behavior rather than a tax on savings. Taxing naïveté may be economically efficient (since these parents are also likely to have the most inelastic savings behavior), but it is hardly equitable and, in the long run, may breed resentment.

Trade-off 2: Targeting Benefits Has Meant Confusing Prospective Students

The current method by which benefits are means-tested requires families to fill out complicated financial aid forms to qualify. Student financial aid is not administered like other forms of means-tested benefits such as food stamps and the benefits of the former aid to families

14. Feldstein (1995).

with dependent children program, for which federal and state governments set up thousands of welfare offices around the country for the sole purpose of helping recipients fill out forms to determine eligibility. Instead, the U.S. Department of Education leaves it up to the students and their families to fill out the complicated application forms. Unfortunately, those who are most likely to attend college anyway will be most successful in surviving the process.

The failure to find an enrollment impact of the Pell Grant program in the mid-1970s may be a result of the fact that those who applied for and received benefits were those who were going to college anyway. This may be an explanation for the success of proprietary schools offering programs in cosmetology, real estate, travel and tourism, truck driving, and so forth in enrolling students. Even though the cost to the students of attending a proprietary school often exceeds the cost of attending a local public community college, anecdotal evidence suggests that the proprietary schools make it much easier to apply for aid. The community college, with large public subsidies from state governments and less dependence on tuition revenue, has much less incentive to recruit these young people.

Trade-off 3: Program Quality Is Difficult to Regulate Directly

The availability of large public subsidies justifies a public interest in the quality and content of postsecondary education. Although it is arguable whether there is a social interest in facilitating investments in occupational skill or fundamental research, the public clearly has no interest in subsidizing entertainment. Yet the potential for abuse is clear when a $3,000 Pell Grant or a $1,500 tax credit is on offer.

This is not a new problem: of the 8,800 schools approved under the GI Bill through 1950, some 5,600 were private for-profit proprietary schools. One of the most troubling episodes occurred in the mid-1980s with the growth of the Supplemental Loans to Students program. Between fiscal year 1986 and fiscal year 1988, after the Supplemental Loans to Students program raised the loan limits for independent students, for-profit proprietary school students increased their share of loan volume from 8.2 percent to 61.5 percent.[15]

Beyond tampering with eligibility rules and loan limits, the federal government has exercised little leverage in directly regulating fraud in

15. Fraas (1990).

higher education. A possible reason is the failure of the regulatory triad made up of the U.S. Department of Education, state licensing boards, and private accrediting agencies to protect federal interests. To receive federal Pell Grants and student loan funds—and now the Hope Scholarship and Lifetime Learning tax credits—an institution must be licensed by the state in which it is located, accredited by an agency recognized by the Department of Education, and be deemed eligible and certified to participate in student aid programs by the Department of Education. However, conducting on-site evaluations has generally been left to state licensing boards and national accrediting agencies. Given that there are primarily federal dollars involved, some states have been less than vigilant in identifying fraud and understandably so. The threshhold to private accreditation seems to require simply finding a group of like-minded institutions. According to Margot Schenet, the number of accrediting agencies grew from twenty-eight to seventy-two between 1952 and 1988. Between 1952 and 1990 no major accrediting agency was dropped from the department's list.[16]

However, it is difficult to imagine ever doing a much better job of direct regulation. First, the federal Department of Education's charter explicitly proscribes any intervention in curricular issues. The values of academic freedom have been given more weight historically than the potential cost savings from identifying fraudulent programs or ineffective pedagogy. Second, there are few outcome measures with which to evaluate such programs. The primary indicator available to regulators—loan default rates— only partially reflects the output of the schools and may largely mirror the baseline characteristics of the students these institutions serve. One might expect the programs to look poor on all these measures even if the value added by the programs is well worth the federal investment.[17]

A third reason many programs are difficult to regulate is simply their size. According to Richard Apling and Steven Aleman, the median fall

16. Schenet (1990). This allocation of responsibilities is not accidental. According to Schenet, the diminished federal role is rooted in the legislation authorizing the department, which prohibits it from "any direction, supervision or control over the curriculum, program of instruction, administration or personnel of any educational institution, school or school system, over any accrediting agency or association."

17. According to Apling and Aleman (1990), the median family income for dependent proprietary school students was $12,000 less than for undergraduates overall and $8,000 less than for community college students in 1986. They are also much more likely to be black (21 percent versus 9 percent of public community college students) and are slightly younger than community college students.

enrollment at a proprietary school in 1988 was 64.[18] Only 25 percent had enrollments greater than 175. Such small numbers both increase the costs of doing on-site visits and greatly reduce any statistical power in attempting to measure program quality by observing student outcomes.

In regulating providers of postsecondary education, there are both type I and type II errors involved: either fraudulent or unproductive programs are not closed or some worthwhile activities are accidentally shut down. The fear of closing worthwhile activities has led to little action. However, because there are a number of alternatives available to students (such as community colleges) to fill that gap, and given the loss of public trust in financial aid programs as stories of abuse emerge, the cost of type I and type II errors is not symmetric: the cost of failing to shut down fraudulent operations exceeds the cost of mistakenly shutting down worthwhile schools. Continued vigilance against fraud, even using the crude measure of high default rates as the primary means of identifying unsuccessful programs, is probably justified.

Medical insurance financing may offer some lessons. Health insurance companies have taken two basic approaches to regulating covered medical expenses. First, to limit the purchase of unnecessary services, insurance companies have taken an increasingly strong role in approving individual procedures. Such a level of intervention would, however, be politically difficult for the federal Department of Education. Indeed, any such intervention in curricular issues would probably run afoul of the department's charter. Second, most insurance policies involve some form of copayment, either as a doctor visit fee or deductible or as a percentage of cost. This last has been the approach most commonly taken in education. In addition to the tuition costs that most students pay, they pay the cost of their time, either in reduced labor market activity or reduced leisure time. The department has created a disguised form of minimum copayment by setting minimum lengths of time required for qualifying programs or by limiting aid to those who are enrolled at least half time in college.

The reliance on time-based copayments is also likely to be tested in the near future if technology fulfills its promise to transform postsecondary education and training. Communications technology will increasingly allow students to take courses from home and over great distances. Under current regulations, one cannot use financial aid pro-

18. Apling and Aleman (1990).

grams unless one is enrolled in an institution where more than half the student body engages in traditional classroom learning rather than distance learning. As it becomes more difficult to impose copayments by requiring a specified amount of classroom time, it might be good to think of other forms of copayments, such as loan financing, that would achieve the same purpose of encouraging families to look for educational bargains while still allowing educational institutions to pursue technological innovation.

Trade-off 4: Across-the-Board Subsidies Are Expensive to Sustain When Demand Increases

As the payoffs to postsecondary education rose, students and families responded. Between 1980 and 1995 the proportion of 18- to 24-year-olds enrolled in college increased by roughly one-third. State budgets were spared some of the pain because the size of the cohorts fell. The number of full-time-equivalent students on campus increased by only 17 percent.[19] However, the same demographic trends that were easing the costs of rising enrollment rates during the 1980s are reversing. In the next two decades the number of college-age youth will increase by more than one-fifth.

Between 1975 and 1995 the population of 18- to 24-year-olds declined by roughly 11 percent nationally, although the decrease was even more rapid in some states such as Massachusetts and Pennsylvania, where the college-age population declined by more than a quarter (table 5-1). Over the next twenty years, however, the number is projected to increase by 22 percent. The increase is even more dramatic in several states such as California, which is facing a staggering 57 percent increase, and Arizona, facing a 42 percent increase. Unless these states are willing to increase dramatically their budgets for higher education, public tuition levels are bound to rise.

A Package of Reforms

With these goals and trade-offs in mind, I turn to proposals for reforming the higher education finance system, moving from incremental reforms to more fundamental structural change.

19. National Center for Education Statistics (1997b, table 186, p. 196; table 200, p.208).

Table 5-1. *Projected Change in Population of 18- to 24-Year-Olds, by State, 1975–2015*

State	Percent change 1975–95	1995–2015	State	Percent change 1975–95	1995–2015
Alabama	–7	7	Nevada	72	46
Alaska	7	40	New Hampshire	–5	25
Arizona	33	42	New Jersey	–19	22
Arkansas	–4	1	New Mexico	8	32
California	4	57	New York	–23	20
Colorado	–6	31	North Carolina	–9	17
Connecticut	–26	21	North Dakota	–26	8
Delaware	–18	21	Ohio	–23	2
Florida	18	33	Oklahoma	–7	9
Georgia	8	29	Oregon	–4	19
Hawaii	–12	36	Pennsylvania	–26	4
Idaho	17	16	Rhode Island	–25	20
Illinois	–22	15	South Carolina	–10	8
Indiana	–17	6	South Dakota	–21	6
Iowa	–25	–2	Tennessee	–6	16
Kansas	–19	15	Texas	13	37
Kentucky	–13	–4	Utah	32	28
Louisiana	–14	9	Vermont	–15	7
Maine	–14	–4	Virginia	–6	21
Maryland	–18	31	Washington	4	29
Massachusetts	–28	27	West Virginia	–16	–19
Michigan	–24	2	Wisconsin	–19	7
Minnesota	–19	15	Wyoming	–6	18
Mississippi	–24	2	District of Columbia	–48	55
Missouri	–17	12			
Montana	–13	2			
Nebraska	–20	9	Total	–11	22

Source: Population projections by state and age from the Bureau of the Census.

Proposal 1: Simplification of the Need-Analysis Formula

During his reelection campaign in the spring of 1996, President Clinton proposed a $1,500 tax credit to "guarantee" access to the first two years of college to all Americans. Although the tax credit was widely criticized by education policy analysts for not being well targeted at low-income youth, the proposal eventually became a centerpiece of the campaign. One reason for its popularity was its apparent simplicity and transparency. Although the administration later proposed a $300 increase in the Pell Grant maximum, it generated much less attention outside the higher education policy community. Because the rules of the Pell Grant program are too complicated, many of those who stood to benefit most from an increase in the maximum would have had a hard time knowing what it meant for them.

The current system in which students must submit an application form before they are told whether they even qualify for federal aid is neither simple nor transparent. It is an outgrowth of a system in which colleges tailored a financial aid package for each student. Even though the advent of the Pell Grant program in 1973 meant that aid was attached to individual students rather than being distributed at the discretion of the institutions, aid packaging and the marketing of federal financial aid programs remain largely in the hands of college student aid administrators. As a result, the process remains shrouded in mystery until each student receives a letter describing the aid award. As a result, a disproportionate share of the aid is likely to be directed at those who had already decided to apply to college. Those who are hesitant about enrolling, those whose behavior the financial aid programs are presumably intended to affect, are less likely to know about available aid programs. Rather than raising the financial aid program generosity, simply lowering the barriers to application may have larger effects on these students without spending additional resources on other students.

The Department of Education has made repeated attempts to simplify the financial aid application form. The National Commission on Cost in Higher Education has urged simplification of the application process. However, there are only so many ways to rearrange 108 data items on the page, and all are likely to be confusing. The application form is complicated largely because the need-analysis formula is complicated. Boiling down the formula to a few basic components could go a long way toward making the forms transparent.

To experiment with how closely a simplified formula could be constructed to replicate the need-analysis formula, I used the data from the 1992–93 National Postsecondary Student Aid Study to replicate expected parental contributions based on just two characteristics: family income and family size. My results suggest that a simple ten-by-ten square table showing the mean expected parental contribution by family income decile and family size would capture nearly two-thirds of the variance in the congressional formula.[20] (Such a method would probably explain more of the variation today because housing assets have been excluded.) In other words, one could come fairly close to the complicated need-analysis formula simply by distributing to high school students a table reporting expected family contribution by family size. Although some families would lose under such an approach (for example, those with more than one child in college) and others would gain (those with more than average assets for a given level of family income), the loss of target efficiency would have to be weighed against the gain in transparency. It is not obvious that the value of transparency would lose in that trade-off.

Dropping the asset test from the federal methodology would also be consistent with simplification. First, including assets in financial aid formulas implicitly taxes savings. Between two families of equal size with equivalent streams of income over time, the family that saves more to send their children to college will be awarded less aid. When public tuition was low, the tax rate on savings was not very important because most families had incomes high enough that they would not have qualified for aid in any case. But as tuitions rise, families are increasingly facing positive tax rates on their savings.

Second, the need to report asset values on the financial aid application is confusing for many parents because such information is not required on federal tax forms. If one only has a simple savings and checking account, a reply may only require a brief glance at a bank statement. But the form also asks families to report the value of a family business or farm, potentially a formidable task.

Third, some assets and debts are taxed while others are excluded, which distorts portfolio decisions. Because home equity is excluded from the federal formula, parents are encouraged to convert their other assets into housing equity.

Instead of basing the financial aid on a limited set of asset indicators for one year, it could be based on a longer period of income, perhaps the average of the last three to five years of family income. This would

20. Using the data from the 1992–93 National Postsecondary Student Aid Study, the R^2 from the regression of the parental contribution from the congressional methodology on a set of dummy variables for each combination of family income decile and family size was .612. A similar method could be used to generate a simplified formula for independent students.

come closer to the goal of distributing aid on the longer-term differences in income without taxing savings directly.[21]

When home equity was dropped from the need-based formula in 1993, the income rates were not raised accordingly. Because higher-income families were more likely to have substantial home equity, this change benefited higher-income youth disproportionately. We need not present a windfall to high-income, high-asset families again. To maintain revenue neutrality with respect to income, the benefit reduction rate on income could be adjusted upward to ensure that higher-income families continue to face the same average expected family contribution.

Proposal 2: Raise the Borrowing Limits under the Student Loan Program

A dependent, first-year student can borrow no more than $2,625 under the federal Stafford Loan program. During the second year, the limit is raised to a meager $3,500. The student's parents can borrow more under the parental loan programs. However, if the parents have liquidity problems themselves (loan repayment begins immediately under the parental loan programs) or if they are otherwise unwilling to borrow, the student may be out of luck. Raising the limit clearly involves some costs: defaults may increase, particularly for those who do not finish their first year of college. But this cost must be weighed against the cost of restricting credit to those who lack access to other forms of credit, such as family savings, to pay for college.

Similarly, student loan eligibility should be extended to those attending college less than half time. As technological advances open up new possibilities for distance education, that growth should not be limited by restricting access to financing.

Proposal 3: Front-Load the Pell Grant Program

Even with the increase in the Pell Grant maximum to $3,000, its real value has fallen by 22 percent since 1980 while tuitions at public post-secondary schools have risen much faster than inflation. The Pell resources could be better targeted to raise the maximum grant for the most price-sensitive young person. David Breneman and Fred Galloway have

21. This is the proposal favored by Edlin (1993).

analyzed the possibility of front-loading Pell Grant spending, making the resources available only to those in their first two years of college.[22] In this manner the Pell maximum could be raised by an estimated $700 to $1,000 with no additional spending on the grants.[23]

The primary advantage of front-loading is to have a larger effect on those hesitating about college entry. There would be costs to such a policy. Although it would reduce the difference in price between attending twelfth grade and attending the first year in college, it would raise the hurdle for those passing from their second year into their third year of college. However, one could expect the sophomores to be less price sensitive than those who might not enter college at all. Whether one encourages a student to complete a first or a third year of college, society gains one more year of schooling. However, when policy encourages an additional youth to try college, society gains the additional option value that comes with the possibility that the student will thrive there. In fact, when Susan Dynarski studied enrollment rates of children who benefited from social security survivor's tuition benefits, she found that the enrollment rates of those who had already started college remained higher even after the program had been terminated.

In previous work with Cecilia Rouse, I have found that about one-third of community college entrants complete less than one semester's worth of credits.[24] For many of these people, college entry is an experiment. However, because they drop out so quickly, it is not a terribly expensive experiment. Front-loading the Pell program funds would allow more of them to discover whether they are college material. For those who decide that they would like to go on in college, the student loan programs will be available to help finance the remaining years.

Proposal 4: Evaluate the Impact of Different Forms of Aid

Despite the availability of considerable public subsidies in higher education, chapter 4 showed that low-income youth often behave as if

---

22. Breneman and Galloway (1996).

23. The maximum is not simply doubled, because a minority of Pell Grant recipients receive grants for more than two years. Breneman and Galloway (1996) evaluated the possibility of front-loading the program when the maximum was $2,340. The front-loaded maximum may be different now that the maximum Pell is $3,000.

24. Kane and Rouse (1999).

their decisions to attend college were limited by their financial position. Observers may all have guesses about the likely effects of different policies, but they are just that, guesses. One can only go so far by analyzing the economic incentives implicit in a policy. Perceptions matter, and parents and students may not always think like good economists when it comes to investing in a college education.

In fact, whether the problem is an aversion to debt or lack of knowledge of the complicated financial aid system or the limits to borrowing under the student loan programs, the source of the constraint is not clear. But the solutions—providing better high school counseling or raising the loan limits or raising the Pell Grant maximum—have very different costs. Currently, there is no empirical basis for claiming that one is more effective per dollar spent than another.

Given the size of the spending at stake, it is time to collect the type of information that would allow a comparison. An experimental evaluation, involving comparisons of different treatments, such as better counseling, and larger grant maximums or different types of loan packages may go a long way in helping to choose the most effective alternative.

Over the past two decades, policymakers have sponsored numerous experimental evaluations of employment and training programs for welfare recipients. More recently, the Department of Labor sponsored an experimental evaluation of the Job Training Partnership Act program. The dollars at stake in these programs are small when compared with the size of public subsidies for higher education: federal spending on employment and training programs for welfare recipients was $1 billion a year following the Family Support Act of 1988; appropriations under the JTPA were less than $2 billion in the early 1990s at the time of the JTPA evaluation. Meanwhile, the Pell Grant program costs $6 billion a year, state and local governments spend another $49 billion in direct subsidies to public institutions, and more than $33 billion of federally guaranteed educational loans are originated each year. Given the magnitude of the public investment at stake, an evaluation of the relative effects of different types of aid is long overdue.

The Department of Education recently funded an experimental evaluation of the Upward Bound program. Created more than three decades ago as one of the original War on Poverty programs, Upward Bound provides grants to four-year colleges and some two-year colleges to provide academic preparation and counseling to local high school students. Two-thirds of program participants are required to be from low-income (family income less than 150 percent of poverty) and first-generation college students. The program serves just 42,000 high school students a year, less than 1 percent of those eligible. Although the program provides much more than financial aid counseling and is often limited to students identified by high school counselors as college prospects, interim results have been promising: students are completing more academic credits in high school.[25] Future reports should provide additional information on college entry. The Department of Education should take a similar approach to evaluating the effects of the larger programs under its jurisdiction and do so in a way that would more readily allow a comparison of the relative impact of dollars spent on different forms of aid.

A More Ambitious Agenda

Every field of policy seems to have its own level of tolerance for dramatic proposals. For instance, as exemplified by recent calls for flat taxes or value-added taxes, tax policy analysts are obviously comfortable proposing major changes in the basic paradigm of federal tax collection. Higher education traditionally has had a fairly low tolerance for such drama. In response to rising voter anxiety, there has been a flurry of incremental reforms in the past few years, such as having the Department of Education serve as the source of capital for student loans. But most discussions have taken for granted two important features of the system: large direct subsidies to public institutions and backward-looking means testing. I want to explore the possibility of loosening both of these constraints.

The reforms already suggested would leave untouched many of the structural weaknesses in our system of financing higher education: the annual confusion surrounding aid applications, the large disparities in tuition between public and private institutions, the difficulty of maintaining low-tuition policies in the face of rising demand, the difficulty of distinguishing between "dependent" and "independent" students at a time when more nontraditional college students consider upgrading their skills. No amount of fiddling will help resolve these problems. More fundamental restructuring would be needed.

25. Myers (1997).

Income-Contingent Loan Repayment

Economists have long been fascinated by the idea of providing loans to finance higher education and having former college students repay them out of their earnings over their careers. Nearly forty years ago Milton Friedman described such a plan in his classic work *Capitalism and Freedom*.[26] The basic idea is to sign a contract with young people as they enter college in which they agree to repay some percentage of their income each year after they leave college. The term of the loan, how long it takes graduates to repay the principal and any interest, would depend on students' income. High-income students would repay their loans quickly, low-income students would take longer and, depending on how large a portion of income the schedule demanded, some people would not ever repay the full value of the principal.

Forcing high-income youth to support loan forgiveness for their low-income peers by paying above-market rates, as has been suggested, is likely to be futile because it would discourage those who anticipate successful careers from participating in the program.[27] If the students who expect the most successful careers opt out, program participation would be limited to a pool of students most of whom would be expecting to receive some loan forgiveness. Therefore, rather than asking fellow borrowers to pay the cost of loan forgiveness, it is more practical to provide the same terms to all students, but allow students to choose the repayment scheme that they prefer later in their careers—with high-income borrowers simply paying off their their loans sooner—and ask taxpayers to pay the cost of loan forgiveness.

Despite its popularity among economists as a means of smoothing a person's consumption over time, there has been no national income-contingent loan option until the Student Loan Reform Act of 1993 required the Department of Education to offer an income-sensitive repayment option to those in repayment under the new direct loan program.[28] After graduating from college, student borrowers were allowed to choose between a standard repayment schedule or the income-contingent repayment. The first cohort of entered repayment in spring 1995.

---

26. Friedman (1962).
27. Bowen and Krueger (1993).
28. The Reagan administration ran a small demonstration program with a version of income-sensitive loans during the mid-1980s. However, the program provided very little loan forgiveness.

The resistance of private lenders, who continue to provide most of the capital loaned out to students under the federal guaranteed loan programs, has been a primary reason there has not been an income-contingent option widely available before now. Understandably, private lenders find the standard repayment plan much more lucrative: the fixed payment model over a relatively short period of ten years is less expensive to administer and ensures a more predictable income stream from their investment.

Under the federal income-contingent repayment plan, any principal or interest unpaid after twenty-five years is to be forgiven. However, default rates are expected to be low, given the relatively high "tax rates" on income. Under current regulations, single students with income of $7,700 or less would pay 55 percent of what they would pay over a twelve-year fixed payment plan. That percentage is raised gradually to 100 percent for single persons with incomes above $36,700.[29] Those with higher incomes—who would otherwise simply pay off their loan quickly—will be allowed to choose to pay no more than they would have to pay under a standard repayment plan. To avoid providing too much of a subsidy to spouses not in the labor force, the joint income reported by married borrowers will be divided between the spouses proportionally to their debts.

Forward-Looking Means Testing

The income-contingent repayment plan has been designed to increase repayment rates and lower default rates. The minimum repayment rates have been set fairly high to ensure that few will end the twenty-five-year period with positive balances. However, an income-contingent program could be designed to target larger federal subsidies toward those with persistently low incomes by setting lower repayment rates and antici-pating a larger proportion of the caseload to reach the twenty-five-year limit without having repaid all of their debt. Policy already targets ben-efits using the backward-looking means testing of the need-analysis sys-tem. Those with low family income at the time they are applying to school will receive a federal Pell Grant no matter what their actual incomes later. An alternative would be to target the resources to those who actually turn out to have less remunerative careers.

29. *Federal Register*, vol. 63, no. 138 (July 20, 1998), pp. 39010–14.

As an alternative to the backward-looking means testing implicit in the current federal methodology, forward-looking means testing would have a number of advantages. First, it would eliminate the very high tax rates on parental savings. Indeed, loan burdens might actually decline when parents have less of an incentive to hide their assets to help pay for their children's schooling.

Second, it would be "taxing" a much longer stream of income in deciding who receives aid, rather than a single year of family income and assets. The use of a broader income base would allow for a lowering of the tax rates.

Third, the distinction between dependent and independent students would become moot. No longer would they have to go through the contortions required to determine expected family contributions for those who do not fit the model of an 18-year-old dependent. Both dependent and independent students would be treated exactly the same and would pay according to their incomes later. One might expect those graduating after the age of 40 to repay at higher rates, given that they can expect to have a career shorter than twenty-five years.

Fourth, student borrowers could be provided with greater insurance in case their careers do not take the expected trajectory. Currently, borrowers receive relief only when they are willing to ruin their credit rating by defaulting or when their incomes are sufficiently low to meet federal forbearance limits.

Fifth, income contingency provides an indirect method for financing on-the-job training after college. Formal schooling is only one option for learning a skill. Much informal training already occurs at the workplace. One would expect workers themselves to be financing any general training by accepting lower wages during periods of training. These same workers have to put food on the table, however, and therefore may face some limit on the amount of training they can finance themselves. On its face a student loan program is primarily a means of financing formal schooling. But on closer inspection an income-contingent loan program, by providing a mechanism for lowering payments with declines in earnings and providing credit at reasonable rates during those periods, is potentially much more than that. For those who have outstanding loans, it also provides a means of financing informal on-the-job training by adjusting payments to current income. Those who graduate from college and want to take a job with low pay now in return for much higher returns later have the flexibility to do so.

Most important, though, because subsidies would be based on a longer stream of income, they would be much better targeted toward those with low incomes after college than for those with low family income immediately before college. Under current law, persons with low-income parents may receive a Pell Grant even if they can expect to be investment bankers on Wall Street. Clearly, this is one of the goals of the program: to provide disadvantaged youth with the chance for distinguished careers. However, a grant is not the only way to give them a chance to go to college. Instead, liquidity could be provided to anyone who wants to attend college, then grants could be given to the most disadvantaged—but based on twenty-five years worth of income, rather than four years worth of parental income while a child is in college.

Paying for Income Contingency

One candidate for offsetting budget savings would be the in-school interest subsidy, which pays the interest on "subsidized" Stafford Loans while students are in school. There are two substantive arguments for using the in-school interest subsidy to help pay for a more generous income-contingent loan program. First, the population qualifying for the subsidy is generally less needy than many other financial aid recipients. Because the interest subsidy is worth more the longer one expects to remain in school, those with lengthy stays in college, who are probably less likely to be hesitant about college attendance, benefit more. Second, there are real costs to tying up society's resources in a college education that is not being used. As a matter of economic efficiency, college students should be forced to take into consideration the cost of lengthy delays. Given liquidity constraints, students probably should not be asked to make payments while they are in school. However, the interest costs could be captitalized with the value of the loan.

There is clearly a large political hurdle to be cleared in using the in-school interest subsidy to pay for greater income contingency in the loan program. In 1995 the Republican leadership in Congress was forced to back down from a proposal to reduce the in-school interest subsidy. But the politics may be different if the cuts are traded off against greater income contingency (rather than a reduction in the capital gains tax). The reason is that there are two groups who benefit most from income contingency. The first consists of those who can expect to have the lowest incomes after they graduate. This constituency is virtually the same one that unsuccessfully supports an increase in the Pell Grant maximum each year. One might think that if they were the only supporters, the proposal could not expect to be any more successful. However, those who borrow more—that is, those attending higher-cost, private four-year institutions—are also more likely to benefit from an income-contingent loan program. Many middle-income youth do not qualify for the in-school interest subsidy because their parents' incomes are too high. Some of these students may expect to benefit along with the low-income youth from an expansion of the income-contingent loan program. Moreover, many more parents and students who will receive little benefit in expectation may actually value such a program to the extent that it reduces the risk of default. Income contingency is comparable to an insurance policy against career difficulties.

An Alternative Route to Income Contingency: Tax Expenditures

As described in chapter 2, the Taxpayer Relief Act of 1997 included a number of new tax expenditures for higher education, projected to cost $41 billion by 2002. One reason for using the tax code to provide these new education subsidies was the same congressional budget rule requiring any increase in discretionary spending to be paid for with cuts in discretionary spending, not with revenue increases. The same revenue increases that were used to pay for the educational tax expenditures in the Taxpayer Relief Act of 1997 could not have been used to pay for an increase in income-contingent loan forgiveness, for instance.

But the tax expenditures also could have been used as a way to provide income-contingent loans. Those with loan payments exceeding some fraction of their adjusted gross income could be provided with loan forgiveness in the form of a credit on their federal income tax return.

An income-contingent tax credit would be easier to administer than the Hope Scholarship and Lifetime Learning tax credits, which now require universities to verify bachelor's degree completion, confirm that a student is either in the first or second year, confirm half-time enrollment status, and collect parents' social security numbers to help the Internal Revenue Service determine eligibility. The National Association of College and University Business Officers estimates that the numerous new verifications required by the Taxpayer Relief Act of 1997 will cost colleges and universities $137 million in 1999.[30] In contrast, the student loan payment tax credit would make use of existing administrative records maintained by the Department of Education and private lending agencies. And because an income-contingent loan tax credit would not affect the loan collection costs of private lenders, the student loan industry may be less opposed to income contingency through the tax system. (Indeed, to ensure industry support, taxpayers could be given the choice of directing the tax credits to their creditors in order to pay down their principal.)

Robert Reischauer offered a more radical approach to using the tax system to provide income-contingent loans.[31] Under his proposal the social security trust funds were to be used to provide the capital financing, and repayment would be financed with payroll taxes. The alternative approach I have discussed would likely generate less resistance among private banks because they would continue to serve as the source of financing. Borrowers would simply report their loan payments and receive a tax credit if the payments exceeded a given proportion of their income.

Conclusion

The changes in the labor market over the past two decades have meant that investing in education is an increasingly important determinant of economic growth. For the same reason, it is also an increasingly important determinant of social mobility. It is ironic that the social and economic future of the country increasingly depends on the economic decisions of college-age youth, a group whose decisionmaking is only slightly less hormone soaked than that of the average high school dropout. Yet rather than making their decisions easier and the costs and benefits of various options more obvious, we have been making the trade-offs more complex as public tuition levels rise and various tax credits affect families' costs in complicated ways.

Unfortunately, we have built a system so complicated that it nearly requires a college degree simply to understand the full range of subsidies available. Although any form of means-testing implies some level

30. National Association of College and University Business Officers, work group 4 (1998, p. 3).
31. Reischauer (1989).

of complexity, much of that complexity is currently situated at the front end of the college application process, taking the form of financial aid forms and complicated need-analysis calculations, rather than later in a student's career. By simplifying the need-analysis formula, front-loading the Pell Grant program to students in their first two years of college, and relying more heavily on income-contingent loan repayments, we can clear up some of the uncertainty currently obscuring youth's vision as they decide about college. While we may introduce new complications for these students later in life—for example, with an income-contingent loan tax credit—the stakes in life are rarely as high as when one is graduating from high school and first choosing a career.

Although college is certainly not for everyone, the rise in economic returns over the past 15 years has justified an increase in society's investment in college. Whether one chooses to enroll in college should depend less on how skillfully one's parents can navigate the system and depend more on whether youth can expect to prosper there.

References

Apling, Richard N., and Steven Aleman. 1990. *Proprietary Schools: A Description of Institutions and Students*. Congressional Research Service (August).

Astin, Alexander W., William S. Korn, and Ellyne R. Riggs. 1993. "The American Freshman: National Norms for Fall 1993." Higher Education Research Institute, University of California, Los Angeles.

Baum, Sandy. 1998. "Is the Strategic Use of Financial Aid to Research Sound Fiscal Goals at Odds with Achieving Equity in Higher Education?" *College Board Review* 186 (Fall): 12–17.

Baumol, William J., and William G. Bowen. 1966. *Performing Arts: The Economic Dilemma*. New York: Twentieth Century Fund.

Becker, Gary S. 1993. *Human Capital: A Theoretical and Empirical Analysis, with Special Reference to Education*, 3d ed. University of Chicago Press.

Bell, Linda. 1997. "Not So Good: The Annual Report on the Economic Status of the Professor, 1996–97." *Academe* 83: 12–20.

Betts, Julian, and Laurel McFarland. 1995. "Safe Port in a Storm: The Impact of Labor Market Conditions on Community College Enrollments." *Journal of Human Resources* 30 (4): 741–65.

Bowen, William G., and Alan Krueger. 1993. "Policy Watch: Income Contingent College Loans." *Journal of Economic Perspectives* 7 (3): 193–201.

Breneman, David W. 1996. *Testimony before the Subcommittee on Postsecondary Education, Training and Lifelong Learning of the House Committee on Economic and Educational Opportunities*. Report 104-62. 104 Cong., 2d sess. Government Printing Office (July).

Breneman, David W., and Fred J. Galloway. 1996. "Rethinking the Allocation of Pell Grants." Washington Office of the College Board (February).

Brewer, Dominic J., Eric Eide, and Ronald Ehrenberg. 1996. "Does It Pay to Attend an Elite Private College? Cross-Cohort Evidence on the Effects of College Quality on Earnings." Working Paper 5613. Cambridge, Mass.: National Bureau of Economic Research (June).

Brouder, Kathleen. 1987. "Parental Attitudes toward Pre-College Planning." *Journal of Student Financial Aid* 17 (2): 5–13.

Bureau of the Census. 1995. *Statistical Abstract of the United States: 1995*.

Burtless, Gary, ed. 1996. *Does Money Matter? The Effect of School Resources on Student Achievement and Adult Success*. Brookings.

Callan, Patrick, and Joni Finney. 1993. *By Design or Default?* California Higher Education Policy Center.

Cameron, Stephen, and James J. Heckman. 1997 (rev. 1998). "Should College Attendance Be Subsidized to Reduce Rising Wage Inequality?" Paper presented at the American Enterprise Institute, May.

Campbell, Paul R. 1994. "Population Projections for States, by Age, Race, and Sex: 1993 to 2000." In *Current Population Reports* P25-1111, Bureau of the Census. Government Printing Office.

Card, David. 1995. "Using Geographic Variation in College Proximity to Estimate the Return to Schooling." In *Aspects of Labor Market Behaviour: Essays in Honour of John Vanderkamp*, edited by Louis N. Christofides, E. Kenneth Grant, and Robert Swindinsky, 201–22. University of Toronto Press.

Carroll, C. Dennis. 1983. "Who Applied for Student Financial Aid?" National Center for Education Statistics, Department of Education (January).

Case, Karl E., and Michael S. McPherson. 1986. *Does Student Aid Discourage Saving for College?* New York: College Entrance Examination Board.

Chapman, Bruce. 1997. "Conceptual Issues and the Australian Experience with Income Contingent Charges for Higher Education." *Economic Journal* 107 (May): 738–51.

Chany, Kalman A., with Geoff Martz. 1994. *Princeton Review Student Access Guide to Paying for College: 1995*. New York: Princeton Review.

Christal, Melodie. 1997. "State Tuition and Fee Policies, 1996–97." Denver: State Higher Education Executive Officers.

Clotfelter, Charles. 1996. *Buying the Best: Cost Escalation in Elite Higher Education*. Princeton University Press.

Cohn, Elchanan. 1970. "Benefits and Costs of Higher Education and Income Distribution: Comments." *Journal of Human Resources* 5 (2): 222–26.

Coleman, James J., and others. 1966. *Equality of Educational Opportunity*. Government Printing Office.

College Board, 1990. *Trends in Student Aid: 1980 to 1990*. Washington.

———. 1997. *College-Bound Seniors: 1997 Profile of SAT Program Test Takers*. New York.

———. 1998. *Trends in Student Aid: 1988 to 1998*. Washington.

Conklin, Kristin, D. 1998. "Federal Tuition Tax Credits and State Higher Education Policy: A Guide for State Policy Makers." National Center for Public Policy and Higher Education.

Conlisk, John. 1977. "A Further Look at the Hansen-Weisbrod-Pechman Debate." *Journal of Human Resources* 12 (2): 147–63.

Council of Economic Advisers. 1997. *Economic Report of the President, 1997*.

———. 1998. *Economic Report of the President, 1998*.

Crean, John F. 1975. "The Income Redistributive Effects of Public Spending on Higher Education." *Journal of Human Resources* 10 (1): 116–23.

Davis, Jerry S., Deborah Nastelli, and Kenneth E. Redd. 1994. *State Funded Scholarship/Grant Programs for Students to Attend Postsecondary Educational Institutions*. Harrisburg: National Association of State Scholarship and Grant Programs, Pennsylvania Higher Education Assistance Agency.

Dick, Andrew W., and Aaron S. Edlin. 1997. "The Implicit Taxes from College Financial Aid." *Journal of Public Economics* 65 (3): 295–322.

Duffy, Elizabeth A., and Idana Goldberg. 1998. *Crafting a Class: College Admissions and Financial Aid, 1955–1994*. Princeton University Press.

Dynarski, Susan. 1999. "Student Aid and College Attendance: Analysis of Government Intervention in the Higher Education Market." Ph.D. dissertation. Massachusetts Institute of Technology, Department of Economics.

Edlin, Aaron S. 1993. "Is College Financial Aid Equitable and Efficient?" *Journal of Economic Perspectives* 7 (2): 143–58.

Feldstein, Martin. 1995. "College Scholarship Rules and Private Saving." *American Economic Review* 85 (June): 552–66.

Fraas, Charlotte J. 1990. "Proprietary Schools and Student Financial Aid Programs: Background and Policy Issues." Congressional Research Service (August).

Freeman, Richard. 1976. *The Overeducated American*. Academic Press.

Friedman, Milton. 1962. *Capitalism and Freedom*. University of Chicago Press.

Gifford, Adam. 1970. "Benefits and Costs of Higher Education and Income Distribution: Comments." *Journal of Human Resources* 5 (2): 227–29.

Halstead, Kent. 1995 update. *Inflation Measures for Schools, Colleges, and Libraries*. Washington: Research Associates of Washington.

Hansen, W. Lee. 1983. "Impact of Student Financial Aid on Access." In *The Crisis in Higher Education*, edited by Joseph Froomkin. New York: Academy of Political Science.

Hansen, W. Lee, and Burton A. Weisbrod. 1969. "The Distribution of Costs and Direct Benefits of Public Higher Education: The Case of California." *Journal of Human Resources* 4 (Spring): 176–91.

———. 1971. "On the Distribution of Costs and Benefits of Public Higher Education: Reply." *Journal of Human Resources* 6 (3): 363–74.

Hartman, Robert. 1970. "A Comment on the Pechman-Hansen-Weisbrod Controversey." *Journal of Human Resources* 5 (3): 519–23.

Hauptman, Arthur M., and Cathy Krop. 1997. "Federal Student Aid and the Growth in College Costs and Tuitions: Examining the Relationship." Paper prepared for the National Commission on the Cost of Higher Education by the Council for Aid to Education, an independent subsidiary of RAND (December).

Heckman, James J., and others. Forthcoming. "Substitution and Dropout Bias in Social Experiments: A Study of an Influential Social Experiment." *Quarterly Journal of Economics*.

Herrnstein, Richard J., and Charles Murray. 1994. *The Bell Curve: Intelligence and Class Structure in American Life*. Free Press.

Higgins, A. Stephen. 1984. "Who Knows and Who Goes: Student Knowledge of Federal Financial Aid Programs and College Attendance." *Journal of Student Financial Aid* 14 (Fall): 19–26.

Hoxby, Caroline Minter. 1997. "How the Changing Market Structure of U.S. Higher Education Explains College Tuition." Working paper. Harvard University (September).

Hoxby, Caroline Minter, and Bridget Terry Long. 1999. "Explaining Rising Income and Wage Inequality among the College Educated." Working paper. Harvard University (April).

Jacoby, Hanan. 1991. "Tuition, Borrowing Constraints and the Timing of College." University of Rochester.

Juhn, Chinhui, Kevin Murphy, and Brooks Pierce. 1993. "Wage Inequality and the Rise in Returns to Skill." *Journal of Political Economy* 101 (3): 410–42.

Kane, Thomas J. 1994. "College Attendance by Blacks since 1970: The Role of College Cost, Family Background and the Returns to Education." *Journal of Political Economy* 102 (October): 878–911.

———. 1995. "Rising Public College Tuition and College Entry: How Well Do Public Subsidies Promote Access to College?" Working Paper 5164. Cambridge, Mass.: National Bureau of Economic Research.

———. 1997. "Postsecondary and Vocational Education: Keeping Track of the College Track." In *Indicators of Children's Well-Being*, edited by Robert M. Hauser, Brett V. Brown, and William R. Prosser. Russell Sage.

———. 1998. "Savings Incentives for Higher Education." *National Tax Journal* 51 (3): 609–20.

———. 1999a. "The Aid Game: The Enigmatic Economics of Student Financial Assistance." *Harvard Magazine* 101 (4): 21–26.

———. 1999b. "Student Aid after Tax Reform: Risks and Opportunities." In *Financing a College Degree: How It Works, How It's Changing*, edited by Jacqueline King. Phoenix: Oryx Press (forthcoming).

Kane, Thomas J., and Cecilia Elena Rouse. 1999. "The Community College: Training Students at the Margin between Education and Work." *Journal of Economic Perspectives* 13 (1): 63–84.

Katz, Lawrence F., and Kevin M. Murphy. 1992. "Changes in Relative Wages, 1963–1987: Supply and Demand Factors." *Quarterly Journal of Economics* 107 (February): 35–78.

Krueger, Alan B., and William G. Bowen. 1993. "Policy Watch: Income-Contingent College Loans." *Journal of Economic Perspectives* 7 (3): 193–201.

Leslie, Larry L., and Paul T. Brinkman. 1988. *The Economic Value of Higher Education*. Macmillan.

Little, Lina, and Jay L. Chronister. 1983. "Self-Reported Public Understanding of Student Financial Aid Programs." *Journal of Student Financial Aid* 13 (1): 29–34.

Manski, Charles F. 1989. "Schooling as Experimentation: A Reappraisal of the Postsecondary Dropout Phenomenon." *Economics of Education Review* 8 (4): 305–12.

Manski, Charles F., and David A. Wise. 1983. *College Choice in America*. Harvard University Press.

McGuire, Joseph W. 1976. "The Distribution of Subsidy to Students in California Public Higher Education." *Journal of Human Resources* 11 (3): 343–53.

McPherson, Michael, and Morton Owen Schapiro. 1991a. "Does Student Aid Affect College Enrollment? New Evidence on a Persistent Controversy." *American Economic Review* 81 (1): 309–18.

———. 1991b. *Keeping College Affordable: Government and Educational Opportunity*. Brookings.

———. 1998. *The Student Aid Game: Meeting Need and Rewarding Talent in American Higher Education*. Princeton University Press.

McPherson, Michael, Morton Owen Schapiro, and Gordon Winston. 1993. "The Effect of Government Financing on the Behavior of Colleges and Universities." In *Paying the Piper: Productivity, Incentives, and Financing in U.S. Higher Education*, edited by Michael McPherson, Morton Owen Schapiro, and Gordon Winston. University of Michigan Press.

Mullis, Ina V. S., and Lynn B. Jenkins. 1990. *Reading Report Card, 1971–88: Trends from the Nation's Report Card*. Princeton, N.J.: U.S. Department of Education, National Assessment of Educational Progress.

Murnane, Richard, John Willett, and Frank Levy. 1995. "The Growing Importance of Cognitive Skills in Wage Determination." *Review of Economics and Statistics* 77 (2): 251–66.

Myers, David E. 1997. "The National Evaluation of Upward Bound: The Short-Term Impact of Upward Bound: An Interim Report." U.S. Department of Education, Office of the Under Secretary (May).

National Association of College and University Business Officers. 1998. "Implementing Information Reporting for the Hope and Lifetime Learning Tax Credits." Working Group Reports.

National Center for Education Statistics. 1995. *Student Financing of Undergraduate Education, 1992–93*. NCES 95-202. U.S. Department of Education (November).

———. 1997a. *The Condition of Education: 1997*. NCES 97-388. U.S. Department of Education.

———. 1997b. *Digest of Education Statistics, 1997*. NCES 98-015. U.S. Department of Education.

———. 1998. *Digest of Education Statistics, 1998*. NCES 99-036. U.S. Department of Education.

National Commission on Excellence in Education. 1983. *A Nation at Risk: The Imperative for Educational Reform*. Government Printing Office.

National Commission on the Cost of Higher Education. 1998. *Straight Talk about College Costs and Prices*. Washington: American Institutes for Research.

Nichols, Albert L., and Richard Zeckhauser. 1982. "Targeting Transfers through Restrictions on Recipients." *American Economic Review, Papers and Proceedings* 72 (2): 372–77.

Orfield, Gary. 1992. "Money, Equity, and College Access." *Harvard Educational Review* 72 (Fall): 337–72.

Organization for Economic Cooperation and Development. 1997. *Education at a Glance: OECD Indicators (1997)*. Paris.

Pascarella, Ernest T., and Patrick T. Terenzini. 1991. *How College Affects Students: Findings and Insights from Twenty Years of Research*. San Francisco: Jossey-Bass.

Pechman, Joseph A. 1970. "The Distributional Effects of Public Higher Education in California." *Journal of Human Resources* 5 (Summer): 361–70.

———. 1971. "The Distribution of Costs and Benefits of Public Higher Education: Further Comments." *Journal of Human Resources* 6 (3): 375–76.

Reischauer, Robert D. 1989. "HELP: A Student Loan Program for the Twenty-First Century." In *Radical Reform or Incremental Change? Student Loan Policy*

Alternatives for the Federal Government, edited by Lawrence Gladieux. New York: College Board.

Rosen, Harvey S. 1992. *Public Finance*, 3d ed. Boston: Irwin.

Rothschild, Michael, and Lawrence J. White. 1995. "The Analytics of the Pricing of Higher Education and Other Services in Which the Customers Are Inputs." *Journal of Political Economy* 103 (3): 573–86.

Rouse, Cecilia Elena. 1994. "What to Do after High School? The Two-Year vs. Four-Year Enrollment Decision." In *Contemporary Policy Issues in Education*, edited by Ronald Ehrenberg, 59–88. Ithaca, N.Y.: ILR Press.

Schenet, Margot A. 1990. *Proprietary Schools: The Regulatory Structure.* Congressional Research Service (August).

Sharkansky, Ira. 1970. "Benefits and Costs of Higher Education and Income Distribution: Three Comments." *Journal of Human Resources* 5 (2): 230–36.

U.S. Department of Education. Various years. *The Federal Student Financial Aid Handbook.*

U.S. House of Representatives. 1997. *Taxpayer Relief Act of 1997: Conference Report to Accompany H.R. 2014.* Report 105-220. 105 Cong., 1st sess. Government Printing Office.

Wallace, T. D., and L. A. Ihnen. 1975. "Full-Time Schooling in Life-Cycle Models of Human Capital Accumulation." *Journal of Political Economy* 83: 137–55.

Winston, Gordon C. 1999. "Subsidies, Hierarchies, and Peers: The Awkward Economics of Higher Education." *Journal of Economic Perspectives* 13 (1): 13–36.

Index

THE BROOKINGS INSTITUTION

The Brookings Institution is an independent organization devoted to nonpartisan research, education, and publication in economics, government, foreign policy, and the social sciences generally. Its principal purposes are to aid in the development of sound public policies and to promote public understanding of issues of national importance. The Institution was founded on December 8, 1927, to merge the activities of the Institute for Government Research, founded in 1916, the Institute of Economics, founded in 1922, and the Robert Brookings Graduate School of Economics and Government, founded in 1924.

The Institution maintains a position of neutrality on issues of public policy to safeguard the intellectual freedom of the staff. Interpretations or conclusions in Brookings publications should be understood to be solely those of the authors.

THE RUSSELL SAGE FOUNDATION

The Russell Sage Foundation, one of the oldest of America's general purpose foundations, was established in 1907 by Mrs. Margaret Olivia Sage for "the improvement of social and living conditions in the United States." The Foundation seeks to fulfill this mandate by fostering the development and dissemination of knowledge about the country's political, social, and economic problems. While the Foundation endeavors to assure the accuracy and objectivity of each book it publishes, the conclusions and interpretations in Russell Sage Foundation publications are those of the authors and not of the Foundation, its Trustees, or its staff. Publication by Russell Sage, therefore, does not imply Foundation endorsement.